CALIFORNIA - WESTERN AMERICANA

# The Big Sur

# The Big Sur

## LAND OF RARE TREASURES

by Floyd Schmoe

615873

Chronicle Books / San Francisco

*To Ruth, with love*

Photographs by Larry Secrist
and William and Ann Bryan

Library of Congress Catalog Card Number: 75-27432
ISBN 0-87701-070-6

Chronicle Books
870 Market Street
San Francisco, Ca. 94102

# Photographic Illustrations

*The Big Sur north from Partington Cove*

# One

## A Place of Wonderful Harmony

Until quite late in the 19th century, the Big Sur was an empty wilderness framed by the rugged coastal ramparts of California's Santa Lucia Mountains, which stretch for 100 miles along the rocky shores south of Monterey Bay. Don Gaspar de Portola, in 1769, first marked the place and stamped it with the Spanish Crown. A year later, Father Junipero Serra blessed the region, raising the Christian cross above Mission San Carlos Borromeo del Rio Carmelo near Monterey. But for these determined explorers, and for all the subsequent Spanish and Mexican governors and settlers, this region was vaguely *"el pais grande del sur"*—"the big country to the south," and they saw little of interest in it. Even the Indians of the region had dwelt mainly in the broad, fertile Salinas Valley to the east of the mountains. Long ago ancestors of these tribes, the Esselens, had lived in considerable numbers along the coast, but the Indians of Fra Serra's time only rarely crossed over the Santa Lucia to camp for a season on the sea cliffs and scavenge on the beaches below.

In the 1840s and 50s, outsiders came to the Monterey Peninsula and began to elbow the Indians and Mexicans aside. First, it was a few Yankee fur traders, whalers and cattlemen. Then, after Captain Sutter found his treasure, thousands of gold seekers hurried to the Pacific shores, followed closely by farmers, lumbermen, fishermen and shopkeepers. This new breed of men and women quickly settled in and built roads and towns everywhere along the periphery of the Big Sur, but *"el pais grande del sur"* remained an untrammaled wilderness, as big and empty as ever.

It was not until 1862 that anyone of consequence really took note of this compelling landscape. That year, Professor William H. Brewer of Yale led a field party of scholars through the Big Sur on a typically belated assignment from the California legislature to survey the state's already ravished mineral wealth. Professor Brewer had begun at Christmas time in 1861 from the sun-baked village (now Los Angeles) of 400 Indians and Mexicans clustered about the already crumbling San Gabriel Mission. Several months later, after traveling slowly up the inland valleys with pack mules, Brewer's party had again reached the Pacific Ocean.

The sighting was probably in the vicinity of Point Lobos, for in a letter to his family, Brewer mentions the groves of Monterey cypress which grew at that time in few other areas. At considerable length, he describes the rugged beauty of the coast and comments upon the abundance of marine life to be found there. "More species could be collected in one mile of this coast," he said, "than in 100 miles of the Atlantic Coast." The field party returned then to their camp in Carmel Valley, where Professor Brewer noted in his journal the magnificent "arbutus trees" (madrone, *Arbutus Menziesii*) which grew on the hillsides. He also commented on the size and abundance of the resident rattlesnakes.

By the end of the 1860s, a few Monterey settlers began pushing south of the bay into the Big Sur wilderness. It is said that an American by the name of Davis was the first to homestead along the Big Sur River and that he later sold his cabin to an Indian named Emanuel Innocenti. A name more likely to ring a bell with contemporary Big Sur visitors is Pfeiffer —Pfeiffer Beach, Pfeiffer Falls, Pfeiffer Big Sur State Park, and Julia Pfeiffer Burns State Park. The precursor of all of these memorials was a certain Michel Pfeiffer, who homesteaded with his family in Sycamore Canyon in 1869.

Partington Ridge and Partington Cove, a few miles to the south of the Pfeiffer parks, derive their names from another early settler, Captain Partington, who, about 1874, wrecked his small trading steamer on some rocks near the mouth of the Big Sur River. When the captain discovered the wealth of redwoods in the canyons and groves of tanbark oaks on the ridges, he stayed to become the first logger of the area. Partington also developed a small industry harvesting the bark of the live oak, which was then in demand as a source of the tannic acid used in tanning the hides of the wild range cattle.

Thus, in the 1870s, the intrepid visitor to the Big Sur might find an occasional sign of human life and enterprise—a rude whalers' camp, the Pfeiffer family compound, a few sheepherders shacks, or a small steamer anchored in a sheltered cove to load lumber, tanbark, and hides for shipment north. (Earlier, there had also been a lively trade in fur seal and sea otter pelts, but by the 1870s the animals had been all but wiped out.) But the settlers in the region remained a small and hardy band, for access to the Big Sur area was only by foot, horseback or the logging steamers. It was not until the 1880s that a rough wagon road gradually wormed its way southward along the ocean cliffs, bringing with it a small number of new settlers enchanted with the landscape and determined to find a way to make the Big Sur their home.

This rude wagon track remained the principal means of access with surprisingly few improvements, until the present Highway 1 was completed in 1937. Since that time and that road, a few hundred people have settled in the area and hundreds of thousands visit it each year. But aside from the highway, occasional fences, and the disappearance of the Indian, the grizzly bear and the condor, the Big Sur shows few of the scars and abrasions so often left on a fragile landscape by modern man. In fact, many of the scattered settlers in the area are still without telephone or electricity, and some of them like it that way.

Although the term "Big Sur" now applies to only the central core of the actual biological region, with the northern and southern boundaries determined more by the life style and psychology of its human devotees than by its geographic features, the ecological boundaries are more broadly defined. The Big Sur, in my view, must include the entire area shadowed and sheltered by the Santa Lucia Mountains, which rise suddenly from the Salinas River valley near its mouth in Monterey Bay, culminate in massive Junipero Serra Peak (5,862 feet) toward the middle of the range, and then taper off southward into a series of rounded hills and isolated rocks strewn between Morro Rock on the coast and San Luis Obispo, 20 miles inland.

Professor Brewer's off-hand but accurate remark about the abundance of marine life along the Big Sur can also apply to the life of the adjoining land. Just as few inshore waters can offer as great a concentration and as wide a range of marine plant and animal life, few other spots on the seven continents can exhibit such a variety and abundance of native species. One small area such as Point Lobos displays within its roughly two square miles more than 300 species of plants, including the unique Monterey pine and Monterey cypress. It also comprises more than 250 species of land and sea birds and a diverse group of mammals ranging from the migrating gray whales, to the resident black-tail deer, to the busy brown wood rats. A complete list of insects, reptiles and marine plants and animals has yet to be made, but it would total hundreds of species.

Many factors contribute to the remarkable biotic complex that is the Big Sur, but its unusual climatic conditions and its physical isolation and variety of terrain are the most significant of these factors. Although one might encompass the Big Sur region by traveling less than 100 miles in a north-south direction and only a dozen airline miles east to west—and, for that matter, somewhat less than a mile of vertical distance—the explorer would pass through at least eight distinct life zones. Indeed, merely traversing the mile of vertical elevation from the Big Sur beaches to the summits of the Santa Lucia Mountains, one experiences as many climatic zones, and consequently as many life zones, as one would see by traveling northward as far as Canada. Of all the major geographical features found around the planet, only the tropical jungle, the barren desert, the deep swamp and the Arctic-Alpine tundras are not represented to some degree within this circumscribed haven called the Big Sur.

The coincidence of this varied terrain lying approximately midway between the frigid Arctic and the tropics; the fortunate circumstance of a warm ocean current brushing the continent at this point; the accident of a powerful fault along the coastline forcing sharp peaks to arise almost out of the sea and cutting off this region from the continental climate —these peculiarities of the Big Sur result in the high humidity, cooling winds, mild temperatures, summer droughts and fogs, and the early rains that create almost ideal conditions for a diverse and burgeoning plant and animal life. This unusual galaxy of life becomes gradually more limited in variety and abundance as one moves down the coast, where the sheltering mountains taper off and the dry, warmer southern continental climate begins to take over. The same is true as one moves north, away from the warm, humid ocean current and into a less mild and drier climatic zone.

*Cypress at Point Lobos*

My wife Ruth and I first came to the Big Sur for none of the reasons which had motivated the Spanish priests and explorers or the Yankee traders and settlers. However, we had much in common with Professor Brewer. Being a biologist by profession, I was burning with curiosity about the rediscovery of the amazing sea otter among the rocks and kelp patches along the Big Sur coastline. Being a philosopher by inclination, I was enchanted by the vastness, the grandeur and the natural perfection of the scene which brought me back year after year.

Ruth, my loving companion through 50 years of adventuring about the world, was not a scientist; but she was, like me, a seeker. What we found in this remaining bit of God's hinterland was the pulsing heart of the earth itself—a place where we could feel the spirit and force which vivifies all creatures and glorifies the planet. So the life of the Big Sur was the reason for this book, and the love of it has been full pay for the years we devoted to the research.

In our explorations of the Big Sur, Ruth and I began with the beautiful, though ecologically less varied, north-south dimension. Along the mountainous eastern border of the Big Sur country, this excursion could be made only on foot or by airplane. On the coast, of course, it is very easily accomplished along Highway 1, which follows the Pacific shore closely. Beginning just below Carmel Mission, we first passed by Whalers Cove. Whalers once set out from this sheltered bay on their hunt for the great gray whale during its annual migrations to Mexican waters.

Beyond Whalers Cove, we visited rocky Point Lobos, with its noisy colony of sea birds, sea lion and sea otter. Then we continued through groves of Monterey cypress and pine to Yankee Point and Malpaso Creek. The name of the latter hints at one of the early hazards of travel in the area. The chaparral-covered hills rose higher above us as we moved south, and the intervening canyons became deeper.

At Granite Canyon, a high concrete arch carries the road almost over the sea, with breakers crashing directly below the bridge. Next came Garrapata ("wood tick") Creek and then Palo Colorado ("redwood") Canyon, where the great sequoias of the Big Sur redwood groves are to be seen. Almost every deep canyon for the next 50 miles boasts a few small groves of these magnificent trees.

At Bixby Creek, 13 miles south of Carmel, the road leaps the canyon

*Lichen covered fence*

mouth on another tall concrete arch. It was from this point in 1937 that the fascinating sea otter was rediscovered after being considered extinct for almost 80 years. Further on, just beyond Hurricane Point, the road drops down almost to sea level and winds between broad beaches and mountainous sand dunes piled high by the forceful prevailing westerly wind—the same wind that gives Hurricane Point its name. Point Sur is on the right, a bold granite promontory at the end of a mile-long sand-spit. A light house, fog horn and radio beacon perch on this barren rock which lies between the mouths of the Little Big Sur and the Big Sur Rivers.

We then turned inland, bypassing Pfeiffer Point and following the Big Sur River into the finest stand of redwoods along the way. Big Sur village and the Pfeiffer Big Sur State Park border the river at about this point. Above the village and park lies 3,710 foot Pico Blanco, third largest peak in the Santa Lucia Range. Beyond Big Sur State Park, the road climbs high again and enters a rugged area of beetling cliffs, hidden coves and dark, forest-filled gorges.

At times, only a low guard rail stands between the highway and a 1,000-foot leap into the sea, and from the frequent turn-outs along the way, we looked down hundreds of feet at totally isolated and unreachable beaches. Fat harbor seals, lazy elephant seals, and bawling sea lions had hauled out here to bask in the afternoon sun; and since the day was calm, we could hear their constant bickering far below us.

The next milestone is Partington Creek and Partington Point. A couple of miles farther south is Waterfall Cove and Saddle Rock in Julia Pfeiffer Burns State Park. This became our favorite campsite, and Anderson Creek, just below, our favorite spot for watching sea otter and the passing whales. For another 40 miles, then, the road winds and twists like a thrown lariat climbing high, dipping low, ducking deep into canyons to cross the frequent streams, and then cliff-hanging by its eyebrows on steep headlands above the sea. It is unfortunate that the road is so steep and narrow and the curves so sharp, for the driver of a car has little opportunity to enjoy the grandeur of this ever-changing view. (On the other hand, were the road wide and straight, most people would drive too fast with greater hazard and even less time to enjoy the charm of the area.)

Some might say the Big Sur ends at Lucia (a combined gas station, grocery store and motel), or at Kirk Creek, where there is a Forest Service campground and the Nacimiento Road joins the highway, or at the Monterey County line some 20 miles farther south. It is largely a matter of feeling. For myself, I did not feel we had left the shelter of the Santa Lucia Mountains and the spell of the Big Sur until we had reached Arroyo de la Cruz (Creek of the Cross) and the white, lime-splattered rocks of Piedras Blancas Point, 80 miles south of Carmel.

The east-west dimension of the Big Sur, because of the sharply changing elevations, is much more varied than the far longer north-south route. There is only one road, the torturous Nacimiento track, which climbs from the mouth of Kirk Creek to the crest of the Santa Lucia and then descends to Jolon in the San Antonio River Valley. The road is not recommended for casual driving, but Ruth and I managed to make the trip across the Santa Lucia on several occasions with no serious difficulties. In doing so, we visited every geographic area, every climatic zone, and every biotic region which makes up this richly varied and beautifully harmonized tapestry of nature.

On our first trip along this route, we began on a hot Sunday morning in May, traveling west across the dry plain of the San Antonio River (a tributary of the Salinas). Along with the intense, dry, 90-degree heat, this area was memorable for its open meadows and groves of giant oaks spread park-like across the broad valley. Shallow streambeds, fringed with cottonwoods and willows, paralleled the road, and gaunt cattle rested beneath the trees beside the few remaining waterholes. Here and there, a stand of gray-green digger pines stood out conspicuously.

An occasional turkey vulture could be seen wheeling high overhead on the warm updrafts, but nothing moved on the ground. We saw numerous small burrows which must have been those of the California ground squirrel, but even these busybodies were at the moment enjoying *siesta* in their cool dark chambers below ground. At one point we stopped to examine an ancient oak and found on a dead branch hundreds of small holes drilled in the rock-hard wood by the acorn woodpecker. This cheerful and frugal woodpecker, with its clown suit of white and black and bright red cap, lives mostly on ants during the hot summer months. In the autumn, however, when the slender acorns of the live oaks ripen and fall, the woodpecker gathers them by the thousands and stores them in these individually carved compartments—like bottles of champagne in a wine cellar.

Moving upward along the gently rising easterly slope, we gradually entered into a denser forest of giant trees: madrones, big-leaf maples, California laurels, and yellow pines. This is the "rain shadow" country, where storm clouds impaled on the highest peaks of the Santa Lucia spill excesses of moisture over the summit ridges. This is also an area of occasional winter snows, herds of black-tail deer and wandering bobcats. On rare occasions, cougars have also been seen, and in recent years black bear have replaced grizzlys in the area.

Dropping down the precipitous western slope of the Santa Lucia, we saw the aspect change dramatically. The zone of upper Sonoran forest ended abruptly, as if we had emerged from the mouth of a tunnel, and immediately there was brilliant light and a vast openness. Looking down from the mile-high summit pass, the breaking surf lay almost at our feet. On a day when there is no wind, one can actually hear the distant boom of surf on the beach, four miles away. Beyond the beach, the view is unbroken, limited only by the curve of the earth and the ability of the eye to see. Actually, the nearest land is Asia, a third of a world away.

Steeply sloping meadows—green in winter and early spring, golden yellow in summer and early autumn—carpet the softly rounded ridges on the western side of the Santa Lucia. Here and there, granite outcroppings break through the lush grasses, and a few stunted pines, with tangles of scrub oak between, vary the monotony of the meadowlands. Gray foxes make dens among these rocks and feed upon the mice, gophers, ground-nesting birds, scaly lizards, rattlesnakes and berries which abound in the area.

Our narrow lonely road now switch-backed down a canyon wall on which solitary live oaks and sycamores climb in scattered ranks. Towering high above them all are small stands of tall and somber redwoods growing from the lower reaches of the canyon. These stream-washed canyons, often spaced a mile or two apart, are evidence of a time long ago when rainfall was far heavier than it is at present. They have shallow beginnings in the high, grass-filled valleys, but gradually they narrow and deepen as they descend the slope. Near sea level, the angle of fall becomes pre-

*Alms Ridge from Nacimiento*

cipitous where rushing water has gouged deeply into the underlying rock.

In the canyons occupied by the Big Sur redwood trees, all is hushed and private. The undergrowth is spare—only the tiny, shamrock-leafed wood sorrel and a few other species of plants and animals have become delicately adapted to the dense shade and the thick layer of duff which through the centuries has accumulated beneath these forest giants. Deer sometimes shelter in these groves, and bandtailed pigeons nest and roost nearby. A red-tailed hawk may use the dead tip of an ancient sequoia as a lookout, but otherwise the redwood society is unique in the predictability and uniformity of its character. Hundreds of species of plants and animals, from fungi to broadleaf trees and from protozoans to birds and mammals, may form the biotic community surrounding the site, but within the grove itself there is found only a select and limited company.

As the Nacimiento Road proceeds toward the sea, it cuts through large patches of chaparral interspersed with rock outcroppings and bits of grassy meadow. The chaparral gives its name in turn to the "chaps," or *chaparejos*, which cowboys wear to protect their legs when riding through the stuff. Like the redwood, chaparral thrives in the fog belt on the western slopes; but unlike the exclusive redwood, the chaparral is a highly cosmopolitan society including many diverse and competing species of both plants and animals. It is a pigmy forest of scrub oak, manzanita, mountain mahogany, and a dozen more kindred species. Here one meets coveys of mountain quail, quarrelsome scrub jays marauding hawks, and, in the autumn, the flocks of wild pigeons which swarm up from the redwood canyons to feed upon the abundant supply of oak acorns and the berries of the manzanita. Long-snouted and low-slung wild boar sows often lead their families of piglets into the chaparral with like intent.

Along this coast, the brushlands often extend right down to the shore, with black sage, wild buckwheat, bush monkey-flower, Douglas nightshade, and other shrubs of the so-called "soft chaparral" actually overhanging the cliffs or slowly retreating from the expanding sand. Most of the campgrounds, parks or homesites along the cliffs and benches above Big Sur beaches are carved out of the chaparral. We ended the motoring portion of our traverse of the Big Sur area at Kirk Creek, where the Forest Service has cleared such a campground on a low headland to the north of the stream. Here, we set up camp in an ideal spot for observing and exploring the remaining two zones of the Big Sur: the beach and the sea.

Beaches along the Big Sur coast are extremely varied, ranging from none at all, as along the sheer granite drops at Kirk Creek or Anderson Creek, to the broad and gently sloping strands such as those at Pacific Beach, Pfeiffer Beach, and the extensive dune-fringed beaches just north of Point Sur. There are also gravel and boulder beaches and, when the tide is out, rocky reefs (Point Lobos and Piedras Blancas Point) which can be walked on and explored. Each of these beaches has a distinctive life of its own.

Of those mentioned, reefs and rocky beaches are the most fertile; for they offer the most protection, even in the roughest seas, for marine plants and animals. Thus, sea weeds, sponges, barnacles, anemone, mussels, abalone, oysters, and many sessile organisms abound in great numbers among these rocks. In addition, within the tangle of weed and the clusters of attached shellfish, such free-moving creatures as crabs, sea cucumbers, snails and small fish find secure shelter. In turn, all of these creatures, attached and unattached, provide food for many of the larger finned, winged, and four-footed inhabitants of the inshore waters and of the reefs, rocks and nearby cliffs and brush.

Sandy beaches are less stable and therefore somewhat sterile. Because sand shifts easily, it offers a poor environment for most marine plants and for many marine animals which must attach to an object for feeding and growth. The sandy beach provides shelter for few plants larger than the single-celled phytoplankton, and only for such mobile animals as clams, tube worms, sand crabs and other even smaller crustaceans—"sand fleas," for example—which can burrow. Regarding the sand fleas, they are dependent upon the sandy beach not only because they can burrow in the soft ground but also because the flat beaches collect masses of decaying kelp, which then serve both as shelter and nourishment for the fleas.)

Many birds patrol the sandy beaches, of course, feeding upon both the sparse resident fauna and the rich bounty of sea weeds and fish cast up by the sea. Occasionally, a giant prize, such as a dead seal or even a dead whale, is washed up on the beach, and then such normally land-based

*Sand Formation, Pfeiffer Beach*

animals as raccoons, skunks and carrion birds will join in the feast. In the past, the grizzly bear was also a beach scavenger. William Brewer recorded the sighting on Carmel Beach of a dead whale being torn apart by a number of grizzly bears, while a gallery of hungry California condors stood waiting their turn.

The most barren beach of all is composed of gravel or small boulders. Such a beach is usually high and steep, and the gravel and boulders roll up and down with every wave, dislodging attaching plants and organisms and actually grinding them as between mill stones. This is, of course, how sandy beaches are formed, but the transitional phase provides an inhospitable habitat for most plants and animals. Yet, even here, there is life of a low order and mostly microscopic in size, dwelling within the wet sediments between the stones. Harbor seals and sea lions also prefer gravel beaches to sand as hauling-out places because sand is too hot on sunny days and both sticky and abrasive at any time.

Beyond the cliff and the beach lies the sea itself—or that restless, sometimes violent edge of the sea with which we are concerned here. Just as on the mountainsides and along the various types of beaches, there are distinct wildlife habitats, so there are within the sea several well-defined life zones, or communities of plants and animals. The ecological law which says that environment is the architect of social structure works equally well at sea as on land.

The most significant aspect of the sea along the Big Sur coastline is undoubtedly its boulder-strewn bottom and rocky border, which makes it an ideal setting for a series of thick, hardy kelp beds and for a rich variety of shellfish. Except for the few sandy beaches, the Big Sur shoreline is mainly precipitous cliffs of granite or basaltic rock. Battered and undercut by the constant pounding of the sea, this rocky shore has broken off from time to time in immense chunks, like icebergs from a polar glacier. The rocks are imbedded in the sandy bottom near shore (many of the larger blocks continue to extend partially above the surface), and these submerged rocks serve as attachment points and anchors for the various algae, other sea weeds, and the sessile animals.

With this fortuitous combination of a rocky shore with its growth of tough weed, the calming effect of the weed patch upon the seas, the shelter and food supply provided by the dense growth, and the amazing collection of associated plants and animals attracted to or dependent on the kelp beds, the Big Sur waters are a unique marine habitat almost as rich in abundance and variety of living things as a tropical coral reef.

Thus far, I have spoken only of the human history and the physical attributes of the area. Add to this now the alchemy brought about by unusual seasonal changes; for climate must be added to physical geography to comprise environment. The Big Sur, as a geographic area, is so cut off by the Santa Lucia range from the climatic whims and caprices of the American land mass—and so completely dominated by the mollifying influence of the warm Asian current with its moist onshore winds—that it is almost oblivious to the seasons established by the conventional calendar.

Here, spring comes in early winter. Summer becomes a sometime thing experienced only on rare afternoons of clear sky and failing wind or during the season the rest of the continent knows as autumn. Winter is confined to the cold summits of the mountain peaks and a few storm-ridden days at sea level. Climatically, then, this is a rare land of almost constant spring, with a brief hot, dry season in late summer and early autumn during which the plants and animals can relax and recoup their energies and resources before bursting out again in exuberant growth. The Big Sur does have its seasons, but they are seasons of drought and rain, sunshine and fog.

Thus, life along the Big Sur can seem ageless, timeless. The earth greens, then fades, then greens again against an unchanging background of rock, mountainside, briny sea and the constant gray of warm, moist, wind-borne fogs. Plants and animals, each in response to the Big Sur and to its own biological rhythms, live their lives and die, never failing at some point in their existence to hand down to the next generation the precious heritage of the past and the hope and challenge of the future. And though neither earth or sky, land or sea, plant or animal give conscious thought to the marvelously complex skein of inter-related and inter-dependent threads which make up the fabric of its being, each unknowingly responds to the needs of the other, so that out of what might otherwise have been chaos and violence and cruelty, a place of wonderful harmonies has evolved.

All other things of nature take this miracle in easy stride. Only one creature, you and I, must ask the how and why.

23

*Moss covered fence, Old Coast road*

*Rocky Creek*

# *Two*

## A Time for Gray Skies and Greening Meadows

W hen winter comes to most other areas of the northern world, spring is already advancing in the Big Sur. And unlike most other areas, the new season does not make its way with such tormenting slowness. Rather, springtime in the Big Sur comes suddenly, like a burst of lightning through rifting clouds, with the first hard rains of December or even of late November.

High on the bald peaks and within the crestline forests of the Santa Lucia, real winter may take hold briefly, with freezing temperatures, occasional snowfall and even the rare blizzard. At the lower elevations as well, there are infrequent but unmistakably wintery outbursts from the Pacific. But as a whole, "winter" in the Big Sur is really the advent of a glorious green and flowered spring. After weeks of heat and months of drought, there is cool water again in the high land springs and streams.

The earth becomes soft, and tender green shoots of native grasses and of wild oats (originally imported by the missionary fathers) spring up overnight in the mountain meadows. Soon masses of flowers, in a hundred forms and hues, weave tapestries of bloom along the shore and across all the lower slopes and meadows of the coastal range. Red-winged blackbirds herald the new season from the replenished ponds and marshes above the sea cliffs. Newborn wooley lambs, with black faces and wobbly legs, proclaim it in joyous bleats from the lush green meadows. Even the plant and animal life in the cool dark depths of the sea somehow sense the coming of spring and move to grow, to spawn, to migrate, to mate—to begin anew the cycle of life and regeneration.

In the chaparral country of the Big Sur, in the season which is both winter and spring, the waxy, cream-colored bells of the manzanita appear almost instantly after the first rains and are quickly followed by edible red or green berries. The common name of this shrub is from the Spanish *manzana*, plus the Latin diminutive *ita*, which together means "little apple." The ponderous Greek generic name—*Arctostaphylos*—refers to the wooly undersides of the manzanita leaves.

Along with the acorns of the scrub oak, the manzanita bushes provide the bulk of the chaparral's bounty for its denizens. Once Indians competed with the grizzlies for the manzanita berries. They dried them in the sun, then pounded them into a paste or flour to garnish their venison, roots and shellfish. They also brewed a medicinal tea from the leaves of the manzanita. Now both the bears and the Indians have gone to the great beyond and mainly wild pigs and pigeons vie for the fruit of the manzanita, although many other birds and animals feed upon these berries.

By February, when the rains have diminished somewhat and the sun is shining more frequently, crinkled new leaves no larger than a mouse's ears are already unfurling on the branches of oaks, alders and sycamores which have only just shed last year's foliage. Soon sulfur-yellow flowers burst open on the big-leafed maple trees, and a dozen other showy blossoms appear overnight: crimson Indian paint brush, golden poppies, dainty blue mariposa lily, blood-red California peonies, tiny yellow violets ("wild pansies").

At the edge of the canyon woods, the shiny-leafed California lilac, or ceanothus, spread a blue haze of sweet feathery blossoms which attract swarms of bees and the earliest hummingbirds. A few weeks later, and higher on the ridges, a closely related species, bearing sweet plumes of creamy white flowers, comes into bloom. Both are especially delicious to the black-tailed deer and, because of this, are often called "deer brush."

In the canyons, beneath the giant redwoods, clusters of dainty wood sorrel bloom with pale pink flowers. Their shamrock leaves, which close at dusk and open again in the morning, are sought by gourmets to lend an unusual and very pleasant sour taste to soups and salads. Another early bloomer within the redwood forest is the giant butterbur, or colts foot, which appears most often along the rushing springtime streams. Nearby, between the moist rocks and mossy tree trunks, maidenhair ferns hang in festoons and the furry fiddleheads of giant *woodwardia* ferns rise one by one to replace last season's tired fronds. Later, the broad and glossy leaves of the sword fern will grow six to eight feet tall.

Nearer the sea, the trees and plants of the forest luxuriate in the continuously moist atmosphere and come to resemble a tangled tropical jungle. In addition to the various broad-leaf trees commonly found in these woods, there are always at least two varieties of wild gooseberry, a blue elderberry and a thimble berry, several species of ferns, and a muddle of vining plants—among them wild morning glories, clematis, honeysuckle, and the tri-leafed poison oak. The latter often climbs as high as 20 feet into the branches of trees.

In the open meadows above Highway 1, along quieter coastal roadsides, on the high sandy benches and dripping sea cliffs, on dunes and fine sand beaches such as those around the mouths of the Big and Little Sur Rivers—everywhere along the coast, the turgid angular leaves of the Hottentot fig (or of other varieties of the so-called "ice plant") form tangled mats that exclude most other vegetation and provide reliable protection from wind erosion. These succulent plants, native to South Africa, have flourished and become a commonplace feature of the California coast. The waxy flowers bloom at all seasons and range in color from white, through varying shades of yellow, magenta and rose. The yellow flowers often turn pink as they age and dry out.

Tall seaside daisies occasionally add dabs and swatches of lavender and blue to the springtime landscape of the Big Sur coastline, but yellow (with the fresh, vivid greens of new leaves and grasses) seems to dominate the area's palette. Beach primroses and beach poppies, though in flower for most of the year, double and triple their display of yellow in the spring. The delicately fragrant sand verbenas also flaunt a special outburst of small, densely clustered yellow (and, occasionally, pink) blossoms in the springtime months. And yet another yellow bloom, the lovely mimulus, or monkey-flower, hangs its masses of golden lanterns over the rocky cliffs.

The only people I know who have actually experienced a bad snow storm in the Big Sur area are Forest Ranger Jim Messick, his wife Polly, and their three small daughters. It was in 1970, on December 18th, and

*Wild flowers*

the Messicks were living at the time in a tiny cabin on a forest camp on Nacimiento Pass along the crest of the Santa Lucia.

"There was little warning," Polly told me. "The sky was dark, but there was no wind. We were snug and warm in the cabin, and all slept soundly until about two o'clock in the morning, when we were startled by a terrible groaning and rending, followed quickly by the crash of the huge madrona tree which stood alongside our house. We looked out then upon a sight that neither Jim nor I had ever seen before. Snow was sifting down slowly and silently in huge wet flakes. All the open spaces were deeply covered, and the horizontal branches of the evergreen oaks, the laurels and the madronas were weighted almost to the ground with the tons of snow. Soon, other of the forest veterans began to fall and large branches were torn from the sturdier trees.

"The noise was like war—like a city being blasted. There were ominous black silences broken at varying intervals by the scream of rending wood and the crash of another forest giant. Hundred-foot yellow pines and centuries-old oaks and maples stood close about the cabin, so that any one of them could have crushed it to the ground. The electricity and telephone were out and the road was blocked. There was nothing we could do but huddle close together and pray."

The Messicks' long dark night came finally to an end. Though the sky was still threatening, the storm had stopped just before dawn, after dropping almost a foot of heavy snow. All about them the forest lay silent and broken. But not a single tree, not even a large branch, had struck the cabin. Fallen trees and branches, now great white mounds, blocked the road.

By evening of the following day, a Forest Service rescue crew with tractors and power saws had broken through to the forest camp and had restored the telephone connection. However, the ranger station and campground had to be closed for several months—first, until the snow had melted and the nearby trees could be removed; then, while flooding from the melt and run-off caused additional damage. The camp is now repaired and operating as usual, but the forest suffered a crippling blow from this rare outburst of winter's fury.

The early spring rains are like a glass of heady wine to the wild pigs of

*Winter on the ridge*

the Big Sur. Unlike domestic pigs, the Big Sur boar, apparently introduced by sportsmen in the 1920s, are mainly nocturnal animals, preferring to feed at twilight or at night and to rest during the day in snug lairs deep within the chaparral. However, the cool waters of the first rains usually bring them out to graze the meadows, even in broad daylight. The earth becomes so soft that rooting and grubbing for the swelling bulbs and tender new roots is an irresistable delight to their porcine hearts. In addition, the rangy sway-backed sows are by then heavy with unborn piglets, so that hunger is gnawing at their bellies.

Good appetites and abundant new growth are a compelling combination. A hungry sow may use her probing snout to plow up a hundred square yards of meadow during a single night. If, as often happens, this "meadow" is the new garden or a prized lawn of a local resident, you can understand how the gentle locals have come to view boar-hunting with some favor. One night at a cottage of friends, a few pigs rooted a large patch below our window, raided the fish pond for water lily roots, and plowed a long trench beside the roadway—and they managed all of this so quietly that none of us was awakened by them.

Since bears have disappeared from the coastal mountains and cougers and bobcats have become rare, the wild pigs of the Big Sur have few enemies except man. With their hefty physiques, nasty razor-sharp tusks, sometimes six inches long, the wild pigs are formidable foes. They have been known to cause serious injury to hunters and their horses (it is common in this rugged country to hunt boar on horseback). I once spotted a distant feeding boar which must have stood almost three feet at the shoulder and was surely more than five feet long and weighed perhaps as much as 300 pounds. It looked, literally, as big as a horse. The California Department of Fish and Game estimates that about 600 wild pigs are shot each year by sportsmen, but this number likely includes many feral pigs as well.

Piglets of the wild boar are usually dropped in March or April while the grass is still green and the roots are succulent. Litters often contain as many as a dozen piglets; and since the gestation period is only four months, two such large litters are sometimes produced by a sow within a year. The piglets are slim, rangy animals, iron gray in color and striped with several light brown ribbons running longitudinally across their sides.

The stripes disappear in the autumn of their first year.

Within a few days of birth, the piglets are following their mothers into the meadows and rooting with their tiny pink snouts as enthusiastically, if not as effectively, as their dams. The young pigs are surprisingly playful, as most young wild things are, and they romp over and around their mothers like clumsy little puppies. At the same time, they are alert and shy and as quick as baby quail to take cover if any threat appears. The sows, while also shy and anxious to avoid trouble, will be bold and vicious in the defense of their young and will charge any man or beast which threatens them.

One warm spring day, Supervisor Bob Freeman of the Julia Pfeiffer Burns State Park, drove a friend and myself up the narrow jeep track which climbs through Partington Canyon to an elevation of about 2,000 feet. In the meadows there and in the tanbark groves nearby, we saw evidence of wild pigs, but it was mid-afternoon and no animals were in sight. It appeared from the size of some of the holes in the ground that the pigs had been trying to dig field mice or perhaps gophers out from their burrows. Pigs, though classed as herbiverous animals, are not at all averse to an occasional meat diet, even carrion.

Later that afternoon, as we dropped down the steep trail which clings to the south wall of the canyon and entered the zone of chaparral, Bob braked suddenly and I looked up to see a whole battalion of little pigs racing down the track in front of us. They were all of a size—no more than a foot long—and the stem-to-stern brown stripes on their sides were quite conspicuous. This was in mid-May; we assumed they were all from one litter.

By chance, no doubt, they formed into three ranks of four each as they made their escape. After a few seconds, as if on a given command of "squad right," every little pig disappeared into the bush below the road. Bob stopped the car and we examined their exit—a well-marked trail less than a foot wide. When we listened, we could not hear a sound. Only the profusion of tiny deer-like tracks gave evidence of their passing. We marveled that so many animals had hit the trail so accurately and then had been swallowed up so quickly and so completely by the brush.

Standing without weapons in the open road and looking suspiciously like "bad guys," we all simultaneously realized that Mamma pig must surely be close by and that she just might be resentful of our presence. We climbed quickly into Bob's four-wheel-drive Scout and coasted discreetly down the steep roadway.

The sea has a constancy (it might even be called cosmic obstinacy) which seems to cradle marine life from the ceaseless climatic changes and hazards in the atmosphere. Wind and rain, day and night, the warmth of spring or the chill of winter exert far less influence over the lives of marine plants and animals than they do over the creatures and plant life of the land. Nevertheless, the seasons, usually for quite different reasons, also affect marine life. There is a vaguely spring-like "blooming" of life in the sea much as there is a "greening" of the land.

For example, due to temperature differentials, to the eastward rotation of the earth, and to the mysterious workings of the moon on the tides, the western coastal waters experience early springtime up-wellings of cool, nutrient-laden waters from the depths. These rich waters, when exposed to the spring sun and warmth, trigger "blooming" among the diatoms and other phytoplankton of the coastal seas. This blooming, in turn, sets off an equal or greater spasm of growth among the zoo-plankton—the minute, drifting marine animals which are dependent upon the phytoplankton for their nourishment and oxygen.

The sea water then becomes a plankton-rich "soup" which is eagerly gobbled up by shellfish, shrimp and small fish. Squid, larger fish and sea birds then gorge themselves on the shrimp and smaller fish. Killer whales, seals and sea lions become fat and content on the well-fed fish. Thus, an ever-swelling chain of new life is set in motion, sweeping through the seas like new grass springing up in a hillside meadow after the first hard rain. Certain of the ocean fish also sense and respond to the changing season by beginning long, exhausting journeys to their ancestral spawning grounds along the cool, rock-bound beaches of Big Sur or in the rain-swollen streams and rivers tumbling from the mountainsides.

Another example of the subtle seasonal changes experienced by marine life can be traced exclusively to the effect of the moon on the tides. In mid-December and again in mid-June, for instance, the moon and sun find themselves on the same axis as the earth. The combined gravitational forces cause unusually large "plus" and "minus" tides

—variations of ten, rather than the normal six feet of difference between the marks. If the shoreline is a vertical cliff, as occurs in many places along the Big Sur coast, these unusual rises and falls of the tides alternately expose and submerge only a few additional feet of rock. But where there are gently sloping beaches, mud-flats or rocky reefs, a minus tide may run out for an extra half a mile or more, exposing many square miles of sea bottom for a few hours. Inevitably, the plants and animals within this no-man's-land between tides must respond in striking ways to their semi-annual exposures to the sun and the atmosphere. Unfortunately, even scientists of the sea as yet know much less than they would like about these dwellers of the strand.

My wife Ruth, our niece Kathy Voorhees, and myself satisfied our own considerable curiosity about the tidepool world on January 9, 1968, when we joined the greedily feasting sea gulls, crows, oystercatchers, turnstones, willets and other feathered friends in a thorough exploration of the reef at Piedras Blancas.

It was semester break for college students and we were returning north after picking up Kathy in San Luis Obispo. When we camped that night at the San Simeon campground (the site of a former whaling station and pioneer trading post on the "Bay of Sardines"), I noted in the tide tables that there would be a minus 1.5-foot tide the next morning at 8:10. I talked my companions into a hasty early morning drive to Piedras Blancas Point, a gently sloping reef on the southern Big Sur coastline. The minus tide meant that the water would recede to a point one and a half feet lower than mean low tide. On a shallow reef like Piedras Blancas, acres of fascinating tide pools and sea bottom would be exposed.

There was a light fog when we rose at dawn. The air was not only damp but chilly. Nevertheless, the onshore wind was already operating to dispel the fog, and all signs indicated a sunny day for our explorations. As we motored north, I became aware of an odd circumstance and remarked on it to Ruth and Kathy. We were seeing quite a variety of birds which the highway seemed to divide into two distinct groupings. Those on the landward side, to our right, were nearly all typical land-based birds, including a great horned owl perched on a telephone pole. The latter was waiting, I supposed, for some car to kill a rabbit or ground squirrel which would supply him with an easy breakfast. There were also red-winged and brewer blackbirds, and several magpies, all noticeably perched on fence posts or roadside weeds to the right.

The seaward side, on the other hand, seemed to be inhabited entirely by shore and marine birds. In one of the extensive meadows between the road and the beach, for example, we spotted a flock of long-billed curlews stalking about on their stilt legs and vigorously prodding the wet grass with their long, down-curved beaks. Where the road paralleled the beach more closely, we saw many gulls and cormorants perched on the wet rocks and here and there a pair of willets or a flock of sandpipers working the kelp-strewn strand. At another point, we stopped on the landward side near a small pond to observe a pair of ruddy ducks attending one another with great affection. The male was a cute little dandy with a pert tail, black cap, white cheek patches and a red waistcoat. (The poor ruddys have a strange handicap—although they fly and swim well enough, they cannot even waddle on land. Their legs simply do not seem able to bear their weight.)

Of course, the highway appears to divide the land and marine worlds —or at least the land and marine birds—only because it is forced by the facts of local geography to follow the borderland between land and sea. Birds never (and animals rarely) allow fences and pavements to limit their range. Still, our observations that morning did graphically illustrate my earlier ideas concerning the effect of geography upon the congregation of plants and animals into more or less distinctive communities. The coastal highway, and the apparent self-segregation of the land and sea birds, also seemed to me to point up the effectiveness of the invisible boundary lines plants and animals draw between their chosen habitats.

Near the turn-off to Piedras Blancas Point, we saw a recently dead coyote beside the road (on the landside!). Like the horned owl, the coyote had apparently been finding easy but grimly dangerous meals among the automobile kill along the highway. We parked in the midst of a field of ice plant, at the foot of the tall lighthouse tower. Following a dim trail to the beach, we noted on the right the two great lime-spattered rocks which give the point its name. Then, after descending a steep bank of recently deposited gravel and conglomerates, we were confronted by the low reef of ancient granite.

This area is prime for abalone picking. For this reason, it is also a rich sea otter feeding ground. During the abalone picking season, which is governed by California law rather than by the sun or the moon, the reef swarms at low tide with hi-booted or wet-suited human predators, each armed with an abalone "gun"—usually a sort of pry bar made from a piece of automobile spring. Fortunately, the abalone season was not yet open, and since the otter preferred to dive for their shellfish rather than to walk over the slippery rocks of the reef, Ruth, Kathy and I, along with the flocks of hungry birds, were the only invaders of the chilly point. Because of the unusually low tide, we were able to walk over rocks normally six to ten feet under water.

The outer reaches of the reef, extending from the land at a two or three degree tilt, were dramatically eroded by wave action into deep parallel ridges and troughs. It was as if the whole reef had been cut into careless furrows by a giant plowman. Each of the furrows contained countless tide pools where small fishes were temporarily trapped while the resident anemone, limpets, snails, crabs and other crustaceans tried to carry on their normal way of life despite their sudden exposure to the cool but dessicating early morning sun and wind. As we scrambled down the reef, being careful of our footing on the weed-covered rocks, I remembered and told Ruth and Kathy of William Brewer's observations of a hundred years ago on the unbelievable abundance of marine life on the beaches and shoreline rocks of Monterey Bay.

On the upper fringes of the reef—the area nearest the shore and routinely accustomed to exposure at "mean" low tide—there were dense mats of black mussels overgrown with patches of goose barnacles and tuft after tuft of eel grass (one of the very few flowering plants that grow in salt water). There were also a few limpets and hordes of periwinkle snails. The latter are given the Latin name Littorina (meaning "shore dwellers") because they live only at the edge of the sea and never actually in it. In fact, these water-shunning animals can often be seen retreating with considerable haste from the advancing tide.

The periwinkles are not, as I pointed out to Kathy, really land forms, though they may be tending in that direction. They are only temporary refugees from the sea, to which they must return to reproduce. In the meantime, to survive, each, like an astronaut in space, carries within its

*Sea urchin and crab at low tide*

spiraled shell a few drops of its natural briny environment. This precious bit of salt water keeps its gills wet and permits the creature to go for days, even weeks, without further contact with the sea.

The periwinkles are so well-protected and self-sufficient in their hermetically sealed shells that they are virtually invincible to most of the creatures that would prey on them. Ed Ricketts, John Steinbeck's "Doc" Watson, told a story of having fed a periwinkle to a laboratory anemone. The hungry anemone swallowed the snail, shell and all. The next day, as Ed had expected, the anemone expelled the shell. However, much to the scientist's amusement and probably the anemone's disgust, the shell was not empty. Like Jonah cast up on dry land by the frustrated whale, the little snail calmly extended its foot and walked away.

In the area below the littoral zone, we found that several seaweeds —the common rock weed and the so-called wracks—took over from the eel grass and barnacles. Swaying in the tidal currents at high water, these fields of brown algae would be lush meadows through which the sea otter would pursue its prey. To us they were drab and slimy patches which made our passage to the tidepools extremely slow and hazardous.

Although tidepools are, in effect, annexed by the open sea at each high tide, they somehow retain their identity as a distinct biotic community. The plants and animals of this surprisingly complex and varied association have adjusted to regular exposure to the direct sun and air and, thus, to extremes of water temperature not known to the organisms of the open water. When we reached the outlying granite furrows of the reef, we found that the most conspicuous plants were bright red coralin algae.

Among the loose rocks on the bottom of the pools, we also found a rich animal life which included little purple shore crabs, hermit crabs, thais (a kind of snail), and the smooth, eel-like blennies, flashing from hiding place to hiding place as we disturbed their establishment. Little sculpins—looking like miniature goblins with their "bull heads" and sharp-spined, wing-like pectoral fins—could be seen in the tiny crevices between and under rocks. Clusters of brown, red and purple ocher starfish seemed to dominate the environment. Interestingly, the brown and purple varieties were more common than the rusty-red or ocher variety from which the species derives its name. Occasionally, a "web-footed" leather star, with its smooth skin and irridesent purple and red markings,

*Tidepool*

clung to the steep sides of the rocks or moved slowly on the shell-strewn bottom. Both the leather and ocher starfish relish the various small, shelled creatures found in tidepools.

The Piedras Blancas Reef harbored unusual numbers of the great green anemone, both in the tidepools and on the rocky ledges overhanging the pools. These brilliant flower-like animals, closely related to the tiny coral polyps, derive their bright color from green algae which grows within the anemone's tissue without any apparent discomfort to the creature. In contrast to the better known lichen, in which two simple plants—an algae and a fungus—cooperate to function as a single entity, this strange miscegenation of algae and anemone is between creatures of two very different worlds.

Ignorance of this fascinating bit of natural history has sometimes caused observers to wonder why beautiful specimen anemone fade to a sickly paleness when kept in an aquarium tank. The reason, of course, is that the dim artificial light is not adequate for the maintenance of the algae, a photosynthesizing green plant. The anemone we spotted in the tidepools were still open and feeding, since the tide had only recently receded. The others, more exposed, were drawing in their tentacles to rest. One of these closed anemone was a bulbous mass as large as a small melon. Expanded, it could easily have been the size of a large sunflower.

From a crevice between rocks, I gingerly extracted a fat cancer crab which, barely six inches across, resisted with a strength that seemed almost equal to my own. I could understand why otter find them difficult to manage. On a nearby rock clung another problem food for the otter—a "gum shoe" chiton which was as large as my foot. The chiton are fairly easily detached from their rocks, but their leathery texture make them tough eating, even for the sharp-toothed seal or otter. Ed Ricketts once decided to eat one but pronounced it inedible even before he got it from the frying pan to his plate.

The gum shoe (sometimes called "gum boot") chiton is the largest of more than a dozen types of this strange species of mollusk. The gum shoe and its cousins are considered odd balls even within a huge family of creatures noted for its various and peculiar forms. (For example, consider the incredible range represented by the tiny rock-boring teredo "worm" and the grotesque sea monsters of the squid and octopus tribe.) Chitons

*Sandstone erosion*

are vegetarians like the limpet and abalone and cling tightly to rocks when not feeding. They have segmented shells (commonly called "sea cradles") which are neatly articulated so that the animal can curl itself into a ball like a sow bug or an armadillo. The shells are usually eight-jointed and beautifully patterned in reds, browns, blues and greens.

Just beside the gum shoe, on the underside of rocks and in crevices between them, Kathy and I discovered a number of abalone, both the smaller black variety and the larger red abalone. These huge snails are usually so overgrown with a tangle of sponges, hydroids, bryozoans and various marine plants that they look more like extensions of the weed-covered rocks than like animals. One has to study the rocks very closely to spot an abalone, though I doubt that the sea otter is ever misled by the camouflage. The interior of the abalone shell, by contrast, is an iridescent sunburst blending all the colors of the rainbow. From the time of the Indians until today, abalone shell has been a popular material for the creation of decorative ornaments.

We picked up several dead abalone shells on the reef and found much evidence that the poor abalone must wage a constant battle against many enemies. Some of the shells had the dollar-sized hole in the crown which is the work of the sea otter's blows. Others had tooth marks along the edges—also, we assumed, the work of the otter. All of the dead shells in the tide pools were riddled by holes and cracks made by parasitic sponges, small teredo-like boring clams, and the larger date mussels, which resemble the more common rock-boring piddocks.

When I examined one abalone specimen carefully, I found pin-head size holes covering almost the entire outer surface of the shell. By counting the punctures within an average square centimeter and then multipying by the measured surface of the shell, I estimated that more than 8,000 little clams had burrowed into, and lived within, the ¼- to ½-inch thick shell. In addition, the shell had scores of large burrows which had been carved out by the date mussels. Many of these burrows still contained the shell of the parasitic mussel.

Both the mussels and their smaller associates enter the abalone shells by excreting an acid which dissolves the calcium carbonate of the abalone's shell. (The larger, less subtle rock-boring piddock actually grinds its way in, like a rotary drill-bit.) For a long time, zoologists discounted the idea that the clams and mussels would use a chemical mode of attack on the abalone shell. After all, the shells of the mussel and clam are also composed of calcium carbonate. The scientists naturally assumed that these little borers would be destroyed by their own tool. However, closer investigation revealed that date mussels and boring clams can protect themselves by secreting an acid-resistant coating around their shells. Nature proves again and again to be, among other wonderous things, a very clever chemist.

After about an hour of splashing about the reef, the three of us had absentmindedly worked our way out to the farthest limits of the low tide. We knew that we would have to retreat soon, but we delayed the return for a few more minutes in order to study the giant red sea urchins. We found the urchins only in the furthest tide pools, which were never drained by even the lowest water levels. Along the rocky banks of these deep pools, we saw the red urchins clinging in such numbers that they were literally walking over each other in moving about. They looked like a tangled mass of huge red cockleburs or chestnut burrs.

The urchins have a triple line of defense. First, they have sharp, moveable, sometimes poisonous spines. Second, and hidden between the spines, there are hundreds of tiny but extremely strong three-jawed pincers. Finally the shell provides a tough armor within which the animal, like the armadillo, can shelter. I showed Kathy that if an urchin is threatened by a pointed object, it will swing its swivel-mounted spines, like threatening lances, toward the point of attack. But if a flat object, such as a man's hand, is brought to bear, the spines will swing away from the point of attack to give the mean little pincers a chance to take hold.

One would assume that with their long sharp spines, grasping pincers and sturdy shells, these not-so-distant relatives of the starfish would have little to fear from predators. However, urchins are a favorite dish of the sea otter, which, as we had seen, can eliminate the urchin's protective spines and shell with a rock. Sea otter along the Big Sur and Monterey Coast ingest so many bits of purple urchin spine, along with the urchin caviar, that not only their teeth but sometimes even portions of their skull bones are stained pink by the sea urchin dye. Sea urchins are also considered a delicacy and a worthwhile prey by some of the larger, hard-mouthed cabezon and groupers, by the urchin's own cannibalistic relatives, the starfish, and even by man in some areas of the world. I have seen the great purple urchins displayed in markets in Mediterranian ports and in the South Pacific, from Hawaii to Southeast Asia. The pink gonads of the urchin are eaten raw and have a flavor similar to, though perhaps milder than caviar.

The urchins, like the chitons and abalone, are vegetarians and feed exclusively upon marine plants. They have teeth and a complicated set of moveable jaws with which they bite off and masticate bits of seaweed before swallowing it. This jaw structure, when found unbroken in a dead shell, resembles the frame of an old-fashioned candle lantern and is appropriately called "Aristotle's lantern." Along with starfish and other members of the spinery-skinned (echinodermata) clan, the urchins also have thousands of hydrologically operated "tube feet," each of which is equipped with a powerful suction-cup "foot." With these feet, they move about, pull clam shells apart, and capture prey. The urchins can also move by pushing themselves along with a rowing motion of their spines.

By the time our trio had finished "bio-reefcombing" among the urchins, the tide had begun to come in and we had to run for it, scattering the feeding marine birds before us. A dozen or more sea otter resting in a nearby kelp patch showed considerable interest in our departure from the reef. They had been waiting for two hours for the tide to drive us away and allow them to return to this rich feast. When we reached the beach, we dallied for a time, looking at shells and driftwood and the long wind-rows of tangled kelp cast high on the beaches by the winter storms.

I showed Kathy that even the decaying seaweed served a purpose in nature, providing warmth, food and shelter for the literally millions of small creatures, chiefly the amphipods ("beach fleas"), which in turn are the principal attraction for the amazing numbers of shore birds we had been observing all day. Amphipods, a Greek word meaning "all around feet," usually have seven pairs of what must be nature's most highly specialized legs. The first pair, like arms, are designed for grasping; the next three pair for walking forward; the penultimate two pair for moving backward; and the last pair, particularly long and stiff, for making world-record leaps. All of these limbs can be used for swimming as well. In addition to being snacks for marine birds, these hoppers are to the sand beach what their related crustaceans (copepods, shrimp and lobster) are to the sea—and what insects are to the land—a busy scavenger horde and an essential link in the ecology of their chosen habitat.

On our way down to the reef at dawn, we had followed a narrow foot path through a mat of succulent ice plant covering all the area between the light house and the beach. There had not been a single flower. Now only a couple of hours later, under a warming sun, the field was a mass of waxy orange and yellow blooms. It was a lovely surprise and a wonderful finish to a fascinating morning.

I saw my first sea otter many years ago on the morning after Ruth and I had arrived at Big Sur for our first visit. It was early May, and we had come for a holiday stay in the cottage of our good friends, Dryden and Margaret Phelps. Their home was high on a spur of Partington Ridge. Above the cottage and to the east of the surrounding grove of tanbark oaks and madronas were green meadows. To the south, the shadowy, redwood-filled canyon of Partington Creek. And below us, toward the sea, a chaparral-covered, fog-nourished slope which dropped precipitously a thousand feet to the rocky beaches.

From a window on the west, we could look directly into the deep bite of Smugglers Cove, and on calm days we could hear the surf lapping on the beaches and chugging into the cove caverns. The morning fogs seldom reached our lofty perch, and on clear days we could see an expanse of blue Pacific bounded only by the far horizon. It was a haven of calm retreat embellished by sunny days and magnificent sunsets.

The Phelps had come down from their Berkeley home to open the cottage for us, and after a pleasant breakfast together, while Ruth and Margaret chatted about household affairs, Dryden had suggested that the two of us go down to the cove and meet "the neighbors." Dryden's enthusiasms run more to the art and literature of the ancient Chinese than to whales, seals and sea otter. But he was aware of my ecological interests, and he was also aware that the sea otter were rare and elusive creatures seldom seen outside of the rugged and inaccessible Big Sur coastline. He had often observed them resting or playing in the kelp patches off Smugglers Cove, and he knew the trail which would get us there.

At the Partington Creek crossing on the highway, we left the car and took a steep trail down some 300 feet to the mouth of the creek. I had noted that Dryden was wearing waterproof pants with rubber boots, and now I discovered part of the reason why. It had rained during the night, and the dense tangle of ceanothus, sage, poison oak and bracken fern which overhung the trail was loaded down with water. I was soon so wet that I didn't even notice the difference when we were wading the swollen creek at the bottom of the canyon.

(A more salient reason for the pants and boots would reveal itself to me the next day, when I awoke with a burning sensation and found my legs covered with the red rash and welts of the worst poison oak infection I have ever experienced. When the affliction became so uncomfortable that I consulted a Carmel physician, he gave me a calamine lotion and dismissed me with this comforting advice: "It's not spread by scratching, you know, so enjoy yourself.")

On the sunny lower slope, rusty song sparrows twittered among the blooms of paintbrush, mimulus and wild lilacs, but at the creek we entered a silent, shadowy corridor of great cottonwood, sycamore and redwood trees. Then, only a few strides further, I stumbled after Dryden into an even darker world—the tunnel which Partington's men had cut through the headland to reach the tiny cove where his lumber schooners were moored.

We came out into Smugglers Cove on a narrow ledge a few feet above the water. The cove is like a bite taken from the face of the headland by some huge sea monster. Actually, the monster is the sea itself, which by constant nibbling rather than one greedy gulp, had eaten a deep sea cave into the cliffside. The roof of the cave had eventually collapsed under the duress of the sea's attack, and the small cove was left. On the ledge where we stood, there were many rounded pot holes which verified that the sea's relentless erosion of the granite is a continuing process.

Several large rocks, awash at high tide, remained from the fallen roof of the cavern, and around and between these a patch of giant kelp was anchored, its rubbery 20-foot fronds glinting green and gold in the morning sun. This kelp (*Nereocystis*) is an annual and the largest marine plant known. It may also be the fastest growing plant in the world. New fronds grow as much as two feet each spring day, and the ultimate length of a single giant kelp plant might reach 100 feet by autumn.

Ann Bryan

*Otter wrapped in kelp frond*

At first sight, nothing moved except the water, which surged in and out of the little cove and rippled the floating kelp. We moved farther out on the ledge until we stood at the extreme northwest lip of the cove. Then Dryden pointed out and I saw the gray, bewhiskered face of an old harbor seal in the midst of the kelp. For another moment the veteran stared at us with round, questioning eyes; then it sank below the surface without a sound.

Donning my field glasses, I finally spotted the creature we had come to visit. What I had previously perceived to be a frond of kelp waving in the breeze turned out to be the webbed hind foot of a sea otter. Through the glasses I could see him rolled into a bundle of kelp and floating on his back. He was scratching his face and ears with his stubby forepaws, while his longer, flipper-like hind legs dangled upward in the air. We soon made out a half dozen more otter resting in the kelp. Apparently, they had all fed and were beginning their mid-day siesta—all, that is, except one.

Dryden and I were studying the somnolent crowd when we suddenly heard a sharp whacking sound just below the ledge. There, passing only a few feet below us, we saw a small female otter. She swam on her back, sculling along between the kelp and the rock, with alternate strokes of her hind feet; her furry tail trailed in the water. I could not see that it was used much in swimming.

The sound which had startled us was the result of her preparations for a late breakfast. She held a large clam between her forepaws, and she was raising the shell high above her head and then striking it sharply and repeatedly against a saucer-size rock lying on her chest. The clam shell finally cracked, permitting the lithesome otter to pick daintily at the contents of the clam with her claws. Throughout this process, she continued to swim along, skirting the inner edge of the kelp patch. When the clam was finished, she tucked her rock under one arm, rolled once to wash away the fragments of the clam shell, and then dived out of sight.

It is likely that in the spring and summer of 1862, when Professor Brewer and his survey party had worked their way northward to Monterey Bay through the Salinas Valley, there were no longer any sea otter left in the bay. Thousands had once populated these coastal waters, but by 1850 American and Indian fur hunters had all but exterminated the herd, along with the southern, or Guadalupe, fur seal. The sea otter Dryden and I had observed that May morning, more than a hundred years later, were the descendents of a very few pair of otter which had somehow survived the slaughter in hidden coves and offshore kelp patches. Only recently, after more than a half-century of rigid protection under international law, were the otter beginning to multiply and re-establish their range along the Big Sur coast.

This bloody saga of the North American sea otter had really begun more than a century before Professor Brewer's explorations. In 1741, Wilhelm Steller, physician and naturalist of the first Bering Expedition across the North Pacific, observed the sea-going cousins of the land otter and gathered a small collection of otter pelts. When the voyage was completed, the pelts reached the fur market in Moscow, bringing the sea otter to the attention of the world for the first time. It was the richest fur that Russian and Chinese merchants had ever seen, and almost immediately the fur came into great demand and was priced accordingly. At the height of the fur trade, when the popular beaver pelts were selling for a mere $2, each sea otter pelt was worth $50 on the Peking and Moscow markets. Eventually, when the shortages began, choice otter skins would sell for more than $2,000 each.

Shortly after Dr. Steller had introduced his trophies to the Russian fur market, ships were outfitted and manned in Siberian ports, and Russian fur traders began to swarm out along the Aleutian Islands and down the North American coast. By the end of the 18th century, as a result of the fur trade, Russia had claimed land as far south as central California and had established colonies on Kodiak Island, at Sitka in Alaska, and at Russian Fort (now Fort Ross), only a few miles north of the Mexican presidio at San Francisco. The black Russian trading ships, sometimes carrying as many as 100 Aleut hunters with their seal-skin kayaks, cruised the entire coast right into San Francisco Bay. The natives of the storm-swept Aleutian Islands were employed—in many cases, shanghied and enslaved—by the Russian traders because they knew how to find and kill the otter most efficiently.

Indeed, the Aleut hunters, in their tiny kayaks, were almost as at-home in the water as the otter themselves. The Aleuts had always killed some otter among the great numbers along their beaches, though for their pur-

50     *Otter clutches rock as tool . . .*

*. . . to break clam shell*

poses, the skin and meat of the seal were far more useful materials.

After 1804, when Lewis and Clark found numerous sea otter at the mouth of the Columbia, American adventurers joined the hunt, sometimes in cooperation with the Russians, though more often in conflict. The slaughter of otter now extended right down to the limits of the otter range in the Santa Barbara Channel Islands. By the 1840s, competition with the Americans and pressure from the Mexican government, along with diminishing returns from the dwindling herds, caused the Russians to withdraw back to Sitka, leaving both the few remaining otter and the harassed *Californios* to the untender mercies of the American invaders. Finally, in 1911, after the fur trade had lost most of its profit and glamor, an international convention was entered into by Russia, Great Britain, Canada and the United States in order to save the decimated herds of both the otter and the Alaskan fur seal. Actually, the sea otter had been included in the agreement as an afterthought—the animal was already considered virtually extinct.

However, throughout the nearly two centuries from 1741 until 1938, when a colony of approximately 100 otter were discovered playing in the surf at the mouth of Bixby Creek in Big Sur, a few pairs and family groups of the glistening brown creatures had apparently persisted unseen in two areas along the American Pacific—in the far reaches of the Aleutian Islands and along the rugged Big Sur coast. That the isolated southern colony of otter was able to survive is due no doubt to a combination of favorable conditions which did not exist at any other point along the 10,000 miles included in their original range. For example, there are no harbors or safe anchorages, even for small boats, along the 120-mile stretch of rock-strewn surf which lies between Monterey Bay on the north and Morro Bay to the south. Also, with whaling, ranching and lumbering interests in the Big Sur largely abandoned after a mere generation or two of activity, there has been little demand for commercial development of the area.

Most important of all has been the broad beds of kelp anchored like a huge log boom along the Big Sur coastline. The two species of giant kelp which make up the bulk of these beds and give them their peculiar character can grow only where there is a rocky shore—or more precisely, a rocky bottom—because such huge plants must have solid attachments in order to survive the constant and often violent wind and wave action. The Big Sur coast provides such an ideal site and the giant kelp grow in jungle-like profusion. The kelp patches, in turn, provide food and shelter for the otter, as well as for a whole community of other plants and animals.

Numerous shellfish, including the abalone, a kind of giant snail, attach themselves to the rocks at the boundaries of the kelp beds and feed upon the marine plants in the vicinity. The sea urchin feeds directly upon the kelp, and a cousin of the urchin, the starfish, prey upon all of the shellfish. Omniverous crabs of several species provide scavenger service to the underwater community. And, lastly, all of these creatures—the crabs, sea urchins and various shellfish—and most especially the prized abalone, serve as the almost exclusive diet of the otter. As for shelter, the entangling kelp discourages the sea otter's natural enemies—the occasional white shark and wandering bands of killer whales—from any trespass. The only other serious threat to sea otter, aside from man, is the sea itself, and the dampening influence of the kelp patches upon the sea saves many of the younger animals from being dashed upon the rocks by storm-driven waves.

Thus, well-fed and comfortable in the lap of the benevolent sea and their kelp rafts, the sea otter go about their daily routines with little regard for season or climate. Only a violent storm can change the daily pattern of their lives. To feed themselves and their young, to groom their thick pelts (which, since they lack the fatty layers of seals and whales, is their only defense against the chilling water), to sleep and feed again —there is little more the otter have to do. This leaves much time for play and love-making, pursuits the otter usually combine.

Although the sea otter is the smallest marine mammal and was one of the last animals to make the return from land to sea, few other creatures have done it more successfully. The seals are more amphibious, the whales more completely pelagic. And whereas both the seals and whales, like most other air-breathing marine animals, are heavy-bodied and sink easily, the otter are buoyant, float readily, and can spend most of their time relaxing at the surface. In fact, otter cannot sink and *must swim down* in order to gather food on the bottom. Thus, the Big Sur and Monterey otter spend all, or nearly all of their time in the water. However, they

Ann Bryan

*Otter showing fur pouch in which food is stored*

also have the option of resting and sunning on rocks and beaches. The northern otter, living in a land of more violent storms and fewer land-based enemies, still go ashore often.

The Big Sur otter are seldom observed on land, and then only for very brief periods. Some zoologists suggest that expectant mothers may come onto the beaches at night in order to deliver their young, but I am convinced, after months of observation, that most, if not all, pups are born in the kelp beds. Pups are born at any season of the year, though most newborn pups have been noted in late spring or summer. Only one is born at a time, and mothers bear their pups only every other year. The young are nursed for upwards of a year and require three or four years to reach maturity.

Since the otter's favorite foods are so abundant in and near the kelp beds, they live almost as easily as the proverbial mouse nesting inside a loaf of bread. Their land-based cousins must travel miles both by water and overland in order to find their daily food; the sea otter needs only to dive a few feet to the sea bottom, or to swim a few yards to the mollusk-encrusted rocks by the shore. Typically, 15 to 20 individuals live together in one kelp bed, though Ruth and I have also found as many as 75 otter rafting together during winter storms in Monterey Bay.

I can't say whether the sea otter's relative safety and easy living accounts for the fact that the species has grown to be several times the size of its land-based relative. Male sea otter are frequently more than five feet long (including a stubby 10-inch tail) and may weigh up to eighty pounds. Female otter average nearer four feet, with a maximum weight of 75 pounds.

A member of the *Mustelidae*, or weasel family, sea otter have the slim body, high hips, broad and somewhat flattened head, and short, fully furred tail characteristic of the group. They are predacious animals, with the small incisors and the long canines of the meat-eaters. However, their wide-crowned molars are adapted to crushing mollusks and other hard-shelled food. Also, unlike many carnivorous animals, they are remarkably gentle and good-natured.

The rather stubby, short-toed forelegs are used very little in swimming. In fact, often as the otter rests or swims idly on its back on the surface of the water, the forepaws are crossed over the chest. Sometimes, when the sun is bright, the otter will hold their forepaws over their eyes to shade them from the glare. When swimming on their bellies, either at the surface or beneath the water, otters will usually hold their forepaws rigidly at the side and extend them only when making quick turns or approaching the bottom. In other words, the forepaws—with their lack of webbing, their heavy pads, and their semi-retractable claws—are used almost entirely as hands in opening shells, holding food, and even in wielding a rock as a tool. In this function, they are remarkably facile.

The hind legs and feet exhibit the greatest adaptation to a life at sea. The legs are long and extremely agile. The paws are fully webbed and have a long outer digit that gives them the appearance of a seal's hind flippers. The claws are more nail-like than claw-like and are not retractable, and the pads are visible only at the tip of the toe. Swimming and diving is accomplished by long sweeping leg strokes and a rhythmic body movement, assisted at times by the strong, slightly flattened tail. A sea otter can swim both under water and on the surface at a speed of six or eight miles per hour. In a burst of speed, either in an emergency or at play, the animals will sometimes leap clear of the water like a porpoise. Most of their travel is more leisurely, however—a beautifully coordinated total body movement through the water that is more insinuation than swimming.

Under the protection of law since 1911, the Aleutian branch of the sea otter (and the fur seal as well) have now come back in great numbers. However, the California sea otters have shown considerably less resilience. Perhaps, with no place to hide when the fur hunters moved through, the survivors were too isolated from one another. The gradual recovery of their small herds have built up to a population of approximately 1200 in the thirty eight years since they were first publicly sighted.

Under the watchful help of "Friends of the Sea Otter," The Sierra Club and Audubon Society, these little sea animals have been defended from attacks by commercial and sports fishermen who are unwilling to share their shellfish resources. Margaret Owings, who lives with her architect husband, Nat Owings, in a Big Sur house that looks almost straight down 600 feet to Seal Beach and a raft of sea otters in the kelp, was the first to recognize that the sea otter needed a Friend. Through constant watchfulness and study, political pressures and education, this group has protected the otters against their human enemies. The sea otters are now under the jurisdiction of the Federal Marine Mammal Protection Commission and it is hoped that their judgement on this issue will safeguard the otters return from near extinction.

Before we left the sleepy otter in Smugglers Cove, Dryden and I had spotted a pair of hunting sea lions, heading south, and three California gray whales passing at a more leisurely pace to the north. The latter were stragglers from the great annual migration to the Arctic, which begins in Baja California lagoons in the spring. Although the huge mammals were well beyond the cove, they were close enough for us to see clearly the patches of barnacles which cover their backs and give them the gray color that accounts for their name.

The California grays (*Eschrichtius robustus*) are one of more than a dozen species of other whales which were once abundant in the North Pacific. All of them were ruthlessly exploited by a whaling industry which, until whaling was outlawed in the United States in 1970, was still hunting down some species of these generally mild-mannered and highly intelligent animals for no better purpose than pet food and fertilizers. Now only the medium-sized California gray, with its plume-like spout and barnacle-encrusted back, is observed frequently along the California coast. The rare sperm whales and the monster blue whales are occasionally sighted, but the smaller fin-back and sei whales, which were the special quarry of California whaling stations, are now very few in number and have learned to live and follow migration routes well away from our shores.

The California gray whale, like the sea otter and the fur seal, was on the verge of extinction until an international agreement in 1947 provided some protection to the species. And more recently, the killing of the gray whale was entirely prohibited by the Mexican and American governments. As a result of these measures, and despite the fact that a breeding female produces only one calf in two years, the herd of grays has responded quickly. More than 10,000 now move north each spring to feed in the plankton-rich Arctic waters. Each autumn and winter, the 40-foot mammals return, swimming more slowly southward to rest, to bear their calves and to breed again in the broad, warm-water lagoons off Mexico. Their migration route covers an incredible 7,000 miles each way.

W. F. Bryan

*A whale "spy-hopping"*

During the height of the whaling industry, in the mid-19th century, land-based whaling stations were in operation all along the southern half of the North American west coast, with three on Monterey Bay, one at Whalers Cove near Carmel, and another at San Simeon Point to the south of Big Sur. During both the north and south migrations of the grays, these stations killed them literally by the thousands. And this slaughter was for their *oil only*. The "bone" of the grays was too short for the uses then in demand, and there was no market for the meat, fertilizer and other products for which other whale species are still being killed by the Japanese, Australians, and Russians.

By 1900, so few gray whales were left from a mid-century herd of 30,000 that the last of the California shore stations were closed. But this was only temporary relief for the whales; for in 1905 the harpoon gun was invented, and with this deadly cannon mounted on a steam-driven "killer-boat," the hunt became profitable again. The whalers continued to pursue the few remaining grays and added to their prey the sei, sperm, blue and humpback whales, which move much faster than the grays and range farther off shore. Modernized stations were built along the coast and the killing increased.

Later, the industry also devised factory ships, which permitted the whalers to hunt, butcher and process the whales while steaming hundreds of sea miles from their land base. With a factory ship lying nearby, the catcher-boats could even enter the Mexican lagoons, where the pregnant cows and young calves were congregated and extremely vulnerable. Only plentiful numbers of the larger and more lucrative blue and humpback whales along the Mexican coast diverted the whalers from the easy pickings in the lagoons, and thus saved the pitiable remnants of the gray herds from extermination.

The whales, like the seal, the dolphin and the sea otter, were once land animals. Of the four groups, the whales and dolphins are the most completely readjusted to a marine life, since they now cannot survive outside of the sea. Their total reversion is probably the effect mainly of time, for they were apparently the first to attempt the change. Among the whales, the California grays were themselves pioneers; in that they are most closely related to a long extinct marine species which is known to have lived more than 30 million years ago. All species of whales retain the

*A barnacle-covered whale's flukes*

W. F. Bryan

five-digit front foot (now modified into a broad flipper) of the land mammals; and in some species, vestigial hind legs are still to be found imbedded in the tissue of the pelvic area. The tail has adapted most to the marine environment, forming into two broad flukes by which the huge animals can propel themselves most effectively through the water.

The grays travel at what would be for us a fast walk or slow jog. Like their cousins the dolphins, they swim just below the surface and break water every two or three minutes for breathing. In the leisure of the Mexican lagoons and again in the feeding grounds in the Arctic Ocean, these breathing breaks often become "spy-hopping" maneuvers by which the animals raise their heads high out of the water, apparently checking on their location or on other animals or objects in the vicinity. During the long migration, however, the whales seem to prefer finding their way mainly by the contours of the ocean bottom. On every fourth or fifth roll, for example, the migrating gray will arch his back and flip his tail for a deeper dive in which he assures himself that he is still following the preferred shallow waters of the continental shelf.

Any dramatic leaps or playful gamboling above the water during the migration is likely to be sex play or the maneuvers of two bulls vying for the attention of a desirable female. About half of the adult cows are heavy with young on the journey southward and are intent only on reaching the warm lagoons where the calves will be born. However, the other half have weaned their latest offspring while in the north and are ready to mate again. Most save their energies for the migration and do their breeding during the Mexican sojourn, but some of the more hot-blooded young males are loathe to wait and may insist on a little competitive shoving among themselves and some affectionate rolls and dives with their chosen mates.

By Christmas, most of the pregnant cows have reached the calving lagoons of Baja California, and the 16-foot, half-ton calves are dropped, tail-first, into the warm Mexican waters. Since whale milk is more than 50 percent fat, the greedy youngsters grow at an amazing rate. By the following autumn, when they are weaned, the calves will have doubled in length and weight. They have learned by then to feed with the adults on the rich provender found at the edge of, sometimes even under, the retreating ice floes of their summer range in the Arctic. Then, back again in the Mexican lagoons on their first birthday, they follow the example of their mothers in plowing furrows through the soft ooze of the sea bottom. By expelling the muddy water through their whalebone filters, the gray whales strain out the small shrimp-like animals which nourish them through the winter.

Gray whales are believed to live as long as 50 years, and each year without fail the grays make their exhausting pilgrimage to the north. The northward trek in the early spring is usually hurried and well off-shore. They are hungry and eager to get back to the greater abundance of the

Arctic waters. The following autumn, all of them fattened and healthy, the grays move south at a far more leisurely pace. They also journey much closer to shore—perhaps because of the rougher seas. Expectant mothers heavy with young always precede in a column, followed by the unmated cows, the old bulls, and then the immature of both sexes. In 50 years of these comings and goings, a California gray whale will cover a half-million miles of sea. Only a few birds—and some commercial pilots among us *Homo sapiens*—ever travel as far in a lifetime.

Aside from a few killings every year by the Arctic aborigines, who are the only men still permitted to hunt the California grays, this species of whale need be wary only of its smaller cousin species, the orca, or killer whales. Sharks, though far more bloodthirsty among marine predators, will seldom attack any species of whale larger than porpoises and dolphins. The orca, however, have no reason to fear the size of their brethren and they prey on injured, young or straggling gray whales. The killer whales travel in wolf packs, appearing suddenly at the side of their prey and pursuing and attacking the poor creature as a team. Being voracious feeders, the orca must also swallow large quantities of fish; but they seem to prefer warm-blooded meat and will attack dolphins, seal, sea otter and even birds in flight. (Ironically, in captivity, the orca are among the most affectionate of whales.)

Much to my regret, I once saw an encounter between a pack of orcas and a young gray. It was early one May morning. I was scanning the sea from a rocky platform at Point Lobos when I spotted a mother gray with what appeared to be a yearling calf passing by about a quarter mile from the shore. I watched the two stragglers for a moment, saw them make their dives and then turned to observe a flock of sea birds.

I didn't even see the initial attack, it was so sudden and rapid. There were five, perhaps six, in the orca pack; and with the predators' quick appraisal of the weakest, they had surrounded the small yearling, cutting it off from its mother. The young whale would be making its first journey north, so this was likely its first encounter with these ruthless "wolves of the sea." Virtually defenseless against the attack, the yearling didn't have a chance.

All that could be seen from shore was a welter of spray, slim black fins cutting the water, and an occasional white belly as an orca rose up out of the water. The explosive spouts of the young gray soon turned to red, for the technique of the orcas is to butt their torpedo-shaped snouts into the huge mouth of a gray and tear out the massive soft tongue. For a long time after the poor whale must have been dead, the orca continued to tear and feed at the carcass. Then they hurried away to the north, searching for other weak members of the migrating grays. The mother whale lingered in the vicinity at the onset of the struggle; but she was helpless, and when blood had begun to flow, I saw her no more.

Later, in talking with park rangers, I learned that the half-eaten carcass of the unfortunate gray yearling had drifted the following day onto the beach north of Cypress Point. The carcass was examined and identified as young, sex unknown, about 25 feet in length. There was evidence that sharks had also fed upon the remains. After making their study, the men had towed the carcass off the beach and out to sea where they hoped it would sink. On the way out they looked back and found a huge, 12-foot shark tearing at the dead whale. Apparently it is quite common for sharks to follow the orca whale packs and, like jackals and hyenas at a lion's kill, clean up the remains.

The month of May that year was a bad time for whales. Several grays and one small pilot whale were found stranded on beaches between Santa Barbara and San Francisco Bay within a period of a few weeks. This was after the big oil spill in Santa Barbara Channel, and conservationists were worried. However, two of the grays were towed to the whaling station at Richmond and examined by scientists who found no direct evidence linking the deaths to oil pollution. Ruth and I were in Monterey at the time, and I drove to Santa Cruz to look at a whale stranded on that beach. Students from the biological station at Moss Landing were also examining it. The whale, a large male California gray, 42 feet long, had been dead for at least a couple of days, but the thousands of barnacles and "whale lice" attached to it were still very much alive. I took some specimens for study.

Barnacles, not really parasitic, require for their life style a firm place of attachment. This is most often a rock, though a plant stem or leaf, a ship's bottom, a drifting log, or even a live whale may serve as well. In the case of the California gray whales, a species of barnacle (*Cryptolepas rhachianecti*) has become so fond of the grays that they survive on no other site. Whether it is the travel experience, the company, or the skin they most love to touch, these barnacles collect on the smooth black skin of the gray whales in such numbers that the whales would not be recognizable without them.

The barnacles on the old bull carcass at Santa Cruz covered, cheek by jowl, perhaps one-fifth of its body. They were especially numerous on the top and sides of the head, on the upper surface of flippers and flukes, and along the back. Mature whale barnacles are up to one inch in diameter and stand about one-half inch high. As they grow, they become imbedded in the skin a fraction of an inch and are very difficult to dislodge. When they die and fall, or are scraped off, the skin of the whale remains scarred and pitted, and it retains its grayish cast.

This species of barnacle is, needless to say, highly specialized. Of the uncounted millions of minute free-swimming larvae which hatch from the eggs shed into the water at spawning time, only those survive that make contact with a passing whale. This must be one of the most desperate gambles of a profligate mother nature. Some of the students at Moss Landing noticed another peculiar adaptation of these crusty creatures —each of the barnacles orient themselves so that they "face" into the slip-stream of water which follows the contours of the swimming whale's body. This position no doubt facilitates the barnacles' feeding as they are carried through the water—like free-loading passengers on a sea-going dining car.

The hundreds of marine hitch-hikers must hinder the movement of the whales through the water, just as weeds and barnacles on a ship's bottom slow its speed. Aside from this nuisance, however, the barnacles do no real damage to the animal itself. Still, they must be an irritant; the gray whales are often seen scraping themselves on rocks or, occasionally, throwing themselves violently into the air, like a cat with a flea bite.

Other species of barnacles occasionally attach themselves to other species of whales, notably the bowheads and the humpbacks, but the California gray seems to be far more subject to infestation. Why other species in the same waters do not attract the barnacles is not known. Perhaps it is because the gray is a bottom-feeder, a slow swimmer and a shore-hugger. The barnacles are not now bottom- or rock-dwelling, of course, but it is likely that their ancestors were.

Gray whales also carry a form of lice which swarm in all the cracks and crevices between the stony shells of the barnacles. The whale "lice" are actually a species (there were two species on the dead bull) of amphipod and closely related to the "sand fleas" or "sand hoppers" familiar to all beachcombers. Whether or not these "fleas" are parasitic upon the whale or upon the whale barnacles, I do not know. Probably on both —certainly they aren't there simply for the ride.

As I have noted, whales have no serious enemies aside from the killer whale and the mechanized whalers. Hopefully, now that man has by covenant agreed to spare a few more disappearing species from the hunt, the wily sperm whales and the great blue whales, the largest animal the earth has produced, may soon return in numbers to American waters just as the gray whales have done. I pray that this will be so. Surely no other of earth's creatures, unless it is the wandering albatross, so completely complement the vastness, the magnificence, the romance and the mystery of the open seas as do the great family of whales.

During several winter stays at the Phelps' cottage on Partington Ridge or at various campgrounds in Big Sur, the weather was for the most part mild. There was frequent rainfall and almost continual overcast, but we had never been present during a really violent ocean storm. But storms do occur in the Big Sur, if rarely, and my story would not have been complete without a description of one. So I was fervently hoping that nature would favor me, on one of our visits, with a foul display of wind and water.

I also had a more serious reason for wishing bad weather on Big Sur. No one seemed to know how it was that the Big Sur sea otter, which never shelter on shore as the Alaskan otter do (or as the local seal and sea lion also do), managed to protect themselves during a violent storm. Seal, sea lion and even whales are sometimes cast upon the shore by heavy seas, but for otter such accidents are rare.

I had always assumed that the Big Sur otter communities must put out to sea, where the rough weather could be endured in relative safety. However, storm or no storm, there are only a few instances of otter being observed a mile or more from land. And these pacesetters have almost always been lone individuals, never a whole raft of otter. Another mystery

65

*Winter storm, Rocky Creek*

was that when the exceptional otter (always young) is found dead on a beach after stormy weather, there is seldom any sign of injury upon the poor creature. My hope was that with a whopper of a winter storm, I would be able to discover answers to these puzzles.

Finally, one year, I was certain that my wish had come true. The weather had been extremely unsettled for about a week, with periods of light rain interrupted by spots of sunshine. Then, a few nights later, a heavy weather front moved inland, bringing dark threatening skies and savage gusts of wind. All night long the rain battered the windows and slashed the oak trees surrounding the cottage. We looked out next morning onto a gray and troubled sea framed by ominous black squalls driving in from the west. Even from the distance of a half mile, I could hear the waves crashing on the offshore rocks and roaring violently into the deep cove.

There were periods of calm when we thought the storm was passing, but then another black wall would rear up over the horizon and race toward the land with the speed and clatter of an express train. Squall followed squall like waves of angry black bombers. Ruth was disappointed—she would have to remain indoors all day. I was delighted, for I could observe the behavior of our raft of furry friends at Smugglers Cove. I ate a hasty lunch, donned boots and oilskins, and hurried to the cove with all the speed allowed by the rain-soaked road and slippery trail.

On emerging from the tunnel through the headland, I faced a scene of wild confusion. Rain pummeled the cliffs in visible sheets, and great green roiling swells rolled across the rocky points of the cove to shatter against the highest ledges. I could not go nearer the point than the concrete base of the old derrick, and even there I did not feel entirely safe. Inside the cove, the water surged thunderously into the sea caves. No other sound could be heard above the angry growling of the wind and sea. Despite my foul-weather gear, I was soon soaked to the skin and smarting from the salt water bracer.

The big kelp patch at the entrance of the cove heaved and rolled like a buoyant carpet, but it did not give way to the swells. In fact, this amazingly tough mat of floats and slender-bladed leaves dampered and calmed the angry masses of the sea water so thoroughly that waves were not breaking inside the cove. Later I found that a few plants had been torn from their anchorage and cast upon the rocks, but only a very few. Seeing the strength and resilience of the fragile leaves, I could believe, as I had read, that small coastal vessels have ridden out a sudden storm by anchoring within large patches of kelp.

No animals, not even birds, were in sight as I studied the floating kelp, yard by yard, with my field glasses. Occasionally, I picked out a tumbled mass of weed and expected to find an otter somewhere within it, but close examination in every case convinced me that none of the otter were to be found in their kelp patch. I then examined the shore, looking behind sheltering rocks or on ledges above the swells, but again, no otter were in sight. Finally, I climbed precariously to the top of the headland, some 100 feet above the cove, and for many minutes swept the open water beyond the kelp for any sight of swimming otter. Except for an occasional wind-tossed sea bird, no creatures could be seen. The storm possessed the day.

Back at the cottage, bathed and warmly comfortable in dry clothing, I built up the oakwood fire on the library hearth. Then I sprawled before it, and while the rain and wind rattled the shutters, I mused about the places where the otter might have taken refuge. I finally concluded that they must in fact remove themselves well off the rocky shore and there ride the swells, singly or perhaps in small rafts, like a flock of ducks. I even imagined them sensibly putting their forepaws over their eyes as they endured a violent sea.

Late that evening, when the storm front had passed beyond the crest of the mountains or had dissipated itself upon the summits, I put on rain gear again and went back to the cove. A strong westerly wind still blew and the waves ran high. Still no sign of the otter. Again, the following morning, I headed toward Smugglers Cove. By the time I arrived at the beach, the sun was shining far out on the gently heaving sea, but the near shore was still in the shadow of the Santa Lucia peaks. Inside the narrow cove, the green water rose and fell rhythmically, with smooth swells perhaps five feet high.

Each time the swells lifted the kelp patch, a number of resting otter bobbed within view. Some were sleeping, many were grooming themselves, and a few moved idly about on miscellaneous business known only to themselves. Occasionally one would dive and return with food to be consumed at leisure, but none seemed unusually hungry or exhausted. Despite the previous day's turbulence (and their mysterious absence), the scene among the otter was as relaxed and normal as any could possibly be. I returned to the cabin somewhat confused. I was convinced that, in this storm at least, the otter had taken safety somewhere outside Smugglers Cove. But I had no real evidence to support my conclusion that the otter passed the stormiest days on the open sea.

Two years later, on yet another mid-winter visit to Big Sur, I found at least circumstantial indications that I was roughly half-right. As I had thought, the otter apparently ride out the storm in the water. But they seem to do so very close in rather than far offshore. And when possible, they seemed to seek the shoreline nearest safe sandy beaches rather than their rocky-shored home waters.

The weather had portended a proper mode for my "discovery" even before Ruth and I had left Seattle for a return to the Big Sur country. Snow was falling in Seattle, and by the time we reached Oregon, the highway was closed under 14 inches of the white stuff. We waited three days, then cautiously made our way across the treacherous lower passes to the Oregon coast. As we approached the shore, we met torrential rains and winds which gusted to 70 miles per hour. At times we were forced to reduce our speed to 20 miles per hour in order to stay on the road. Lighter cars with trailers, and pickup trucks with high campers had been driven off the road.

The storm continued to follow us south. We spent a rainy night at Sausalito and, early on a Sunday morning, crossed a swaying Golden Gate Bridge from which all light or tall vehicles had been barred. We reached Monterey by noon—just in time to watch four inches of rain, one-fifth of the entire yearly average, fall on the city that day. The wind still blew ferociously, and we heard on the weather report that an unusual frosting of snow had covered all of the higher hills in the coastal range.

We also learned from the radio weather summary that the blizzard we had passed through in Oregon was the southwestern outburst of a wide cyclonic disturbance centering in Western Canada. Strong winds generated by this low pressure area had swept cold air from the far north to circle widely over the Gulf of Alaska and then swing back in gale force against the coast of Oregon and Northern California. As this cold front

*Point Sur in rain*

met the warm air from the southeast, the torrential rains and snowfall, the violent winds and the heavy seas were created. According to the report, the highways of Oregon and Washington were still blocked by snow drifts.

We pressed on cautiously to the Big Sur. Curiously, the wind now blew out of the southeast and was rather warm. At Seal Beach, 30 miles below Carmel, at least 200 seal and sea lion had scrambled to the highest reaches of the sand. They were extremely agitated and the roaring of the big bulls could sometimes be heard over the roar of the surf. At Smugglers Cove, it was simply unsafe to venture beyond the mouth of the tunnel. In any case, nothing was in sight but the dark green sea swirling high upon the rocks and dashing spray a hundred feet into the air. The water in Waterfall Cove heaved like huge bubbles in a boiling caldron. At Anderson Creek, long gray 20-foot combers struck the sheer rock walls, climbed another 50 feet, and then thrust a heavy spray over the brink of the cliff 80 feet above.

Awed and exhilirated by the violence of the storm, we drove on to Kirk Creek Camp. The rain had ceased here and rusty song sparrows were singing. The unseasonally warm air was like Hawaii on the windward side, and the huge green waves reminded me of the giant combers which roll into Oahu's Sunset Beach. Since the sea cliff at Kirk Creek is only 50 feet high, it would have been foolhardy to approach the fence in search of the otter. Instead, after making camp, I walked through the battered shrubbery to the long beach north of the camp ground. From there I could scan the incoming waves at a safe distance.

Low in the west, the sun broke out beneath the cloud cover, and long slanting rays of dim yellow light bounced along the crest of the rolling sea. Near the beach, where the waves curled and crested at alarming heights, the sunlight revealed to my great surprise a half-dozen or more otter swimming in silhouette among the breaking waves. I could never see all of the creatures at one time—there may have been many more than the six or seven I counted bobbing like corks on the flailing water.

Some rested on their back, while others paddled dog-fashion in the water. If a wave broke with an otter on it, the nimble mammal would dive through its crest and appear again beyond the white foam. Some were even coolly grooming themselves as they rose and fell in the surf. Although they were all active, rolling and tumbling and paddling about, none seemed to be struggling in order to remain off shore. The waves simply lifted them and passed them by, then raced onward to crash with the roar of thunder upon the steeply shelved beach.

Where were all the other otter of the Big Sur during that tremendous storm? We never learned, although we were told in Monterey that a large number of the otter colonies had apparently moved into the deep and sheltered Monterey Bay for the winter. On our own, Ruth and I counted more than 70 in one raft off Hopkins Marine Station, and an equal number appeared to be sheltering near Point Pinos, a few miles to the west.

We had solved no zoological mysteries, then—at least not by the rigorous standards of science. But after getting thoroughly drenched and chilled on several occasions during several winter storms over several years, we had at last satisfied ourselves that we knew how the otter handled bad weather. Swimming and floating in the rough seas just beyond softly sloping sandy beaches seemed so eminently sensible for these agile marine mammals that I felt rather foolish for not thinking of it sooner. We were fully convinced now—until someone comes along with a better answer—that the otter must sense the approaching storm and head in small groups for the nearest bay with "beach frontage."

The sky cleared by nightfall, and we slept beneath a star-lit canopy such as city dwellers seldom see. The nearer stars burned brightly in delicate shades of blue, yellow and red, stating boldly their confidence in the established order. Myriad lesser lights of dim whites and grays twinkled and glowed in the background, inviting wonder as to the width and breadth of that distant world. Around midnight the waning moon leaped brightly from the crest of the Santa Lucia and moon craters near the terminator stood out vividly, sharpened by their own shadows. I thought of the little Russian-built wheeled robot creeping along those crater rims, then of the three American astronauts who were that day already on their way for a stroll upon the dusty gray crust. At that moment, when I had just spent the day looking for sea otter in a storm-tossed surf, the idea of men walking about the moon seemed too absurd to be imagined. Later, a bright planet—I think it must have been Venus—appeared above the mountain crest and followed the moon along the zodiac.

At 6:30, when I awoke again, a pink glow had spread across the southern sky and the stars had faded to only a few of the boldest. But the moon still shone like burnished silver in the west; and sister Venus, if it was Venus, stood high and unblinking and bright as a beacon in the southern sky. I dressed quickly and went to the edge of the cliff. It was then 6:45 and just light enough so that I could make out the notes I was writing. Looking down through a thin wisp of fog, which lay like fluff upon the beach, I could see the dim outlines of the rocks a hundred yards from shore. The seal and sea birds which make these rocks a resting place had not yet returned from their storm shelters on land. In the shadow of the cliff, a slight shimmer of light—the luminousity of millions of tiny bioluminescent organisms—outlined the froth of surf as it slid across the hard-packed sand of the beach.

By seven, the pale pink of the southern sky had deepened to orange, and in the west a lighter blue revealed the horizon. A solitary willet pattered back and forth at the edge of the spume, prodding the sand for morsels of food. As I turned back toward the campground, a warm east wind brushed my face and left behind it the pungent odor of sage mixed with the balsam of budding cottonwoods. I could clearly see the higher ridges of the Santa Lucia, changing quickly from mauve to fawn and then to gold as the first yellow light of the sun bathed the snowy peaks. The storm had passed; a glorious new day was breaking.

Over the past few years, a dozen otter pups have been found on California beaches following heavy storms. Vern Yadon, director of the Natural History Museum in Pacific Grove, picked one up alive on the beach near Point Pinos and took it to the Steinhart Aquarium in San Francisco. A game warden found another half-dead on the beach near Hopkins Marine Station. Almost all of the lost pups survive only a few days in captivity. However, I was told of one rescue with a happier ending.

On an evening of brisk wind and turbulent surf, Leland Lewis, whose home faces the beach just north of Point Lobos, heard what he first mistook to be the sounds of a sea bird in distress. He bundled up and went outside to investigate, but no bird was in sight. Then, looking into the boiling surf near shore, he saw a baby otter struggling desperately to

*Sunset, Little Sur River*

keep its head above water and calling frantically for help. Wading up to his waist in the foam and barely able to keep his footing among the erratically breaking waves, Leland finally managed to scoop up the half-drowned otter and carry it ashore. While the frightened little creature squirmed desperately and cried loudly for its mother, Leland squired it quickly to the warmth and shelter of his kitchen.

Mrs. Lewis wrapped the weeks-old otter in a warm blanket and soothed it with gentle words. Amazingly, it soon ceased to cry and struggle. Then with a trusting look in its round black eyes, it began to suck on Mrs. Lewis' finger. Leland telephoned for advice and help and fortunately was able to reach Judson Vandevere, naturalist and lover of sea otter, who arrived shortly after with his young son Keith. Judson devised a formula, which the baby eagerly took from a nursing bottle, and then the tired and contented armful settled down to spend the night curled up with Keith Vandevere inside his sleeping bag on the beach.

Once in the dusk of evening an adult otter, undoubtedly the mother, appeared about 10 yards offshore and called. But before Judson and Keith could return the baby to her, she had disappeared. By morning the wind had dropped and the sea was somewhat calmer. With the help of scuba-diver neighbors, the lost pup was returned by paddleboard to the offshore kelp patch.

Left there on a tangle of seaweed, the baby resumed its pitiful cries for help. It was not long in coming. Within 10 minutes or less, the onlookers heard the mother's responses to the cries. Then they saw the adult otter rise out of the water just a few feet from the kelp. She looked, dived closer and swept the pup off the kelp patch—all in the blink of an eye. The Good Samaritans onshore applauded happily as the mother swam hurriedly back toward the colony with her baby held tightly in her arms.

By May in the Big Sur, the days are hot and the pace of life has slowed. The black-tailed deer and the wild pigs rest in the brush during the day and venture into the meadows for food only at dusk. Dusk is also the active hour for the quail, which lead their coveys of chicks from the shelter of the chaparral into the tall grasses of the meadow. Rodents, too, emerge from their cool burrows to partake of the meadow's bounty. And above all of this activity, silhouetted against the gradually darkening sky, is the lone red-tailed hawk, its keen eyes alert to the movement of its quarry.

By May in the Big Sur, though it is still spring by the calendar, the summer has begun and there are already signs of an approaching autumn. Berries have ripened on the madrone trees. The wild oats and barley grass in the high meadows are a golden yellow. A few dry leaves begin to collect on the ground, and flowers fade on the ceanothus bushes. At the same time, the lower, seaside forests and meadows are still decked with green turf and late-blooming blossoms—a gift of lingering freshness brought by the coastal fogs which are now beginning to roll in off the Pacific each morning and bathe the slopes in moisture.

*Autumn sunlight*

*Fog below Partington Ridge*

# *Three*

## The Summer Fogs

Summer on the Big Sur is determined more by the sea than by the calendar, marked more by dense and chilly mists than by "seasonal" weather. The cool morning fogs are certainly the most characteristic indication that the summer months of June, July and August have come to the Big Sur. These summer fogs are also a most significant factor in the year-long ecology of the area. They keep the lower slopes moist, green and productive for weeks longer than the upper meadows. They determine the growth patterns and life styles of the area's plants and animals. They are the key to such unique West Coast wildlife communities as the chaparral and the redwood groves. They are an integral, inseparable part of the Big Sur experience.

Heat differentials in the air and water generate the famous summer fogs along the Big Sur as well as along all the coastal countryside (and cityscapes) to the north. The phenomenon begins with the existence and presence along the California coast of the warm-water *Kuro shio*, the Japanese Current. This great river within the ocean, akin to the Gulf Stream in the North Atlantic, flows in a northerly direction along the coast of Asia, sweeps the warm water eastward across the Pacific and then drifts southwestward again along the western shores of the United States. At this point in its course, the ocean stream is called, naturally, the California Current. It is also characterized, without nationalism, as the North Pacific Stream.

Ocean streams are powered not by gravity, as are land waterways, but by the eastern rotation of the earth, which causes a westward drift in the

*Fungus on pine, Ventana wilderness*

waters at the equator. This equatorial drift sets up a circular, clockwise rotation of the northern oceans, with a corresponding counter-clockwise surge south of the equator. Because of this circular movement, the North Pacific Stream is already beginning to veer away (southwestward) from the shores of the continent just as it reaches Northern California. And since the immense and powerful stream does not hug this shoreline, vertical currents, bringing cold bottom water to the surface, are formed along the coast.

Now we have most of the elements that produce the fog—the warm California-Japanese-North Pacific current, the eastward rotation of the planet and the westward drift of the central oceans, and the sly vertical currents sweeping cold bottom waters up to the surface along the California coast. Add the hot summer sun, prevailing westerly winds, and the sweltering, mountain-bounded Central Valley of California, and we have created a misty brew. Each summer day the sun-heated air absorbs and holds great quantities of moisture from the tropically warm waters of the California Current. This warm, moisture-laden air drifts across the cold bottom waters nearer the shore. The warm air is then chilled, and the vapor condenses into fog.

But for the hot Central Valley and the prevailing wind, this fog might simply squat stoutly just offshore, keeping land temperatures moderate but permitting bright blue and sunny skies. Indeed, there are rare, sun-blessed mornings in the summer when exactly this arrangement has occurred. One can see the wall of fog, far offshore, waiting for a boost. However, this happens only when the Central Valley is enjoying a few hours of relief from its routine 90- and 100-degree summer temperatures. With its normal hot dry weather, the valley air sets the prevailing westerly winds in motion, drawing the cool offshore air across the coastal mountain range. Of course, as the cool air moves inland, the fog bank follows.

Along the rugged Big Sur coast, the fog nestles against the Santa Lucia range and then creeps upward to 2,000 feet or more over the brush-covered slopes and through the wooded canyons. Along low river valleys or sea-level inlets, such as Monterey or San Francisco Bay, the dense, ground-sweeping clouds may drift much further inland. Usually, by noon the heat of the sun reflected from the hillsides has warmed the dry upper air streams, which then absorb, or "burn away," the fog.

In population centers, such as Monterey and San Francisco, it is difficult for people to endure the chilling dampness of the summer months without complaints. Monterey can be colder on a foggy August morning than on a calm December day, and these conditions are inevitably frustrating for the well-bundled citizenry, who are never really able to reconcile their peculiar weather with our ancient cultural and linguistic identification of the summer months with warmth and constant sunshine. Fortunately, the people find other compensations: fine harbors, beautiful vistas, fertile valleys, mild winters and a rich and abundant economy.

Because the dry season in California is a long one, stretching from May until November, most plants in the open, generally waterless chaparral are deep-rooted, slow-growing woody shrubs and vines which form into a kind of dry and dusty pygmy jungle. Many of the plants have also developed specialized devices for trapping and holding the meager moisture that reaches them through the daily summer fogs. For example, the leaves (through which most plant moisture is lost) are characteristically evergreen and thick and leathery, with a waxy, waterproof covering on their topsides (or the side most exposed to the sun). The tough, often thorny or grasping branches are usually matted into all but impenetrable tangles which, again, help to shelter the leaves from the sun and trap the morning mists. On the undersides of the leaves, the stomata (through which plants breathe) are usually protected by a dense mat of wooly hairs, or by specialized cells which cause the leaf to curl and close its pores when the inner tissue is losing too much water by evaporation.

A dozen species of flowering plants, shrubs and small trees are found in a typical patch of chaparral scrub. Near the edges, the pink-flowered wild buckwheat, sage and sticky mimulus abound. This area is termed the "soft" chaparral by botanists; it is the connective tissue between the meadow and the thicket. As the tangle thickens with mountain mahogany, manzanita, ceanothus, and California holly, the *chaparro*, or scrub oak, begins to appear. This miniature tree—really no more than a shrub—is responsible, of course, for the name given to this type of forest.

Acorns from the scrub oak, the manzanita berries, the cherry-like fruit of the holly and, in late summer, the various fungi provide the main fare which has attracted an entire community of feathered and furry dwellers

*Fog in trees, Burns Creek*

to these bushlands. Succulent roots, worms and insect larvae, numerous wild berries, a carpet of tasty seeds and, of course, all of the small prey which feed and are eaten in the chaparral—food is abundant in these dusty thickets. The shelter is also exceptionally good. The larger animals are more secure from human hunters, who have difficulty cutting through the brush. The smaller creatures, and the young of the large ones, are easily hidden from flying and stalking predators in the tangled, thorny mass of vegetation.

A summer day in the chaparral is likely to be ghostly in the morning mists, hushed and somnolent under the afternoon sun, spiced with sage, manzanita and other aromatic plants as the evening cools. In the gray morning light, a pair of long-tailed California thrashers, several Bewick's wrens and a whole sorority of wrentits stir about the bush, twittering, feeding and preening. When the fog lifts toward noon, the birds become even more vocal and active—especially when they are joined by two equally impudent and quarrelsome jays, one a white-fronted scrub jay, the other the darker, black-crested Steller jay. Yellow-billed magpies drop down from the upper meadows to feed on berries, and a solitary black phoebe, dressed in its nun's habit, appears from beyond the canyon rim to snatch invisible gnats from the air.

A pair of redtailed hawks have staked exclusive claim over a wide area of the surrounding chaparral and meadow, and while the hen may be brooding her spotted eggs on a rude platform of sticks in a nearby tree, the male can be seen watching over their range from the dead tip of a tall tree at the crest of the ridge. A pair of dainty, brightly marked American kestrel, hardly bigger than blue jays, are permitted to work the same area for small birds, lizards and insects. But no other large hawks would dare invade the reserve of these fierce redtails.

Masses of frothy, turquoise-blue ceanothus flowers almost smother the chaparral during the spring, and if any still remain despite the summer drought, dainty Allen's hummingbirds will be hovering nearby, sipping the sweet nectar. In summer, these fascinating little winged dynamos must lean more on insects to feed their growing young. They also seek out the late-blooming yucca flowers. On a warm August afternoon, I have counted dozens of hummingbirds swarming about a single stalk of the yucca's waxy flowers.

At dusk, the perambulating creatures begin to stir. Little brush rabbits appear by ones and twos, nibbling grass and tender leaves beside the trails and never venturing far from shelter. Families of wild pigs remain bedded deep within the thickets throughout the day, the rabbit-sized piglets poking and nuzzling their sleepy mothers. But at dusk the mothers stealthily lead their brood out along well-worn paths to browse and root in the soft chaparral and the meadows. One or more pair of California quail is likely to be found in every patch of chaparral, and late in the day the busy little hen will be seen leading a covy of nine or ten fluffy brown chicks into an open space. There they stretch their legs and stubby wings, dust themselves, and learn to feed. The cock, his black knight's plume drooping gracefully over his forehead, will be standing lookout from some nearby shrub.

The nocturnal denizens of the chaparral now begin to range. Among them are the special favorite of most people, the raccoon. Although raccoons are plentiful and their tracks are to be found in the Big Sur along every stream, on the beach, and even on dusty trails high on the ridges of the Santa Lucia, Ruth and I did not often see the masked bandits themselves. They stay well-hidden during the day and are extremely stealthy in their wandering and feeding after dark. However, one particularly dry summer, when water was scarce, we were treated to a nightly parade of raccoons to the lily pond beside the entrance to the Phelps' cottage on Partington Ridge. There were only a few small goldfish and perhaps an occasional frog in the pond, so we were certain that the coons came not for fishing but merely to wash their food in the water. It was probably the only water nearby. Every night for several weeks we would hear them chattering to themselves or to one another.

This habit of "washing" food, even of washing a perfectly clean ear of corn in a muddy creek, has long caused amusement and wonder to people. In Japanese, the raccoon is called a "washing bear." Naturalists now say, however, that this behavior is not a mark of fastidiousness. Rather the animals lack adequate salivary glands and therefore need the moisture in order to properly masticate their food. Still, I have watched raccoons scrub a carrot vigorously with their little hands, and it looked very much like washing to me. I also watched a pet raccoon scrub a crust of bread until it had all dissolved away, leaving a very puzzled little coon.

During a stay at the Phelps' cottage, we were also awakened once in the middle of the night by a family quarrel on our roof. A bit later we watched the coons amble off into the tanbark—mama in the lead, four cubs in a row, and the disgruntled father trailing behind. On another occasion a raccoon came to the big picture window which looks out over the sea, put her hands against the glass, and looked into the lighted room. Ruth, on all fours, crept to the window, and the two of them then rubbed noses through the glass for a surprisingly long time. They can be bold creatures.

Raccoons are also extremely clever. A friend and neighbor of ours kept a bowl of cat food at the back door and was not particularly surprised when she returned home late one night to find a pair of raccoons finishing off what was left of the cat's supper. Being an animal lover and encouraged now by the evidence that a family of coons was occasionally paying a call, she began to put out extra food for the nocturnal visitors. Thereafter, she found that the water faucet near the back door had been left running a couple of times, but she was not prepared to believe that her new pets were smart enough to turn on the faucet. Some nights later, however, she was awakened by a commotion in the kitchen and got up to find that the raccoons had entered through the cat door, taken a box of corn flakes off a shelf, dumped it into the kitchen sink and turned on the water. They had departed by the time their hostess had reached the kitchen, but they had neglected to turn off the water. It was an unholy mess.

A shy relative of the raccoon, the ringtail cat, is encountered far less often along the Big Sur, though it may well be equally common. Only once did we see a wild ringtail by daylight and that was early in the morning. Hurrying home from a night of hunting, it ran across the trail a few feet in front of us, paused only a moment to look, then melted silently into a tangle of sticky mimulus and wild buckwheat. Only a little larger than a gray squirrel but with a longer tail, the ringtails are weasel-like in their appearance and movements. They also readily climb trees, and in this they more closely resemble a squirrel. There are seven black bands around the bushy gray tail, which is almost as long as the body. Unlike the black bands of the raccoon's tail, the rings do not quite completely circle the tail and the tip of their beautiful "bush" is always black. With the large round eyes of a night hunter, and a pert fox-like face, the little ringtail is a beautiful animal.

Ringtails range along the west coast of the continent from Central America to Southern Oregon. They are seldom found far from water, but they seem to spend less time in it than raccoons do. Though they can enjoy a wide variety of foods, including insects, acorns, wild berries, domestic fruits and the eggs of ground-nesting birds, they feed mostly on mice and other small animals. *Cacomixtles*, "bush cat," the Aztecs called this creature. It is sometimes also called the "miner's cat," because little "caco" was often kept as a mouser in the gold miner's mountain cabin. The ringtail makes a poor house pet or zoo exhibit, however, because it sleeps all day in its den. In captivity they have been found to be extremely fond of honey, but I have never known them to hunt wild honey as bears and some birds do.

A favorite prey of the ringtail cat, and another rather lovable night-walker of the chaparral, is the wood rat. I have had considerable, I might say intimate knowledge of wood rats in mountain camps from Canada to Mexico: I have found them nesting in our woodbox in Glacier National Park, in our attic in a cabin on Mount Rainier, and in an ancient cliff dwelling in the Southwest. In desert areas, I have seen their nests in cactus tangles; and in the forest, a family of the big-eyed, long-tailed rodents had moved into an abandoned beaver lodge. In the Big Sur, at our camp above Waterfall Cove they occupied the neighbors' woodpile. In spite of the fact that they have driven me to distraction and stolen me blind over the years, I have come to develop a certain respect (not to say admiration) for the little pests.

Their nuisance value has been well-established and well-documented. In our mountain cabin they kept us awake all night by their inclination to move things about the attic and their maddening habit of drumming on the floor with their hind legs while deciding what to move next. At times we thought they were trying to move the kitchen stove. For some unfathomable reason, wood rats also have a compulsion to carry things around with them. They seem to feel no great attachment to their impedimenta; for if another object attracts their eye, they quickly drop whatever they have and take on the new toy.

I can testify from infuriating experience that if a camper should be so careless as to leave his watch, his spectacles or his set of teeth beside his bed at night, he is very likely to wake up next morning to find a very nice pine cone, a pretty pebble, or even a hefty chunk of horse dung left in

85

their place. Then he has merely to locate the culprit's nest in order to find the treasured item, more than likely stashed away with a collection of sticks, buttons, table ware, stones, string, nuts, coins, cones—in short, a collection of odds and ends which would rival a peddler's pack or a boy's pocket. In some areas, the wood rats are called "trade rats" or "pack rats" because of their peculiar and inexplicable habits.

The wood rat (family *Cricetidae*) with his alert manner, big round ears, snowy white bib and hairy tail, has none of the loathsome characteristics we attach to the common rat. He holds no threat to anyone—in fact, he is a winning little fellow. He is also good-natured and he is more a collector of trash than a consumer of garbage. Sadly, his chief contribution to the economy of the wild seems to be to raise large families which will feed the owls, hawks, coyotes, bob cats, ringtails and rattlesnakes of the area.

If one were to judge the relative abundance of the various animals in the Big Sur by the remains of those found dead on the highway, he would perhaps have to say that the most common animal is the little striped skunk. However, this is not really a good method of census, since animals seem to differ greatly in their propensity for being mid-highway at the wrong moment. After years of observing frightened animals in my head-lights at night and of stopping many times to identify carcasses on or near the pavement, I have come to this conclusion: Rabbits and squirrels, though very alert and active, are hit frequently because, like chickens, they so often change their minds in the middle of the road. Deer have difficulty with traffic mainly at night, when they are blinded and confused by the bright lights. Skunks are frequent victims because they have one-track minds and pay no attention to anything beyond their immediate concern.

Particularly in the west, the highway department often places "Deer Crossing" signs along the pavement at points where deer commonly cross, but this is not so much for the safety of deer as for the occupants of the car. Many fatal accidents are caused by drivers striking or trying to avoid deer on the highway. It seems to me that there are places where "Skunk Crossing" signs ought to be placed as well, although I doubt if it would do much good. Once near Laramie, Wyoming, we saw such a sign, and the bodies of five skunks which had been killed within the day proved that it was of little help, at least to the skunks.

Two species of skunk are found along the beaches, the canyons and the chaparral of the Big Sur. They are the big California striped skunk and the little spotted skunk or "civit cat." A number of cases of rabies are attributed to skunk bites each year.

The larger, striped skunk may be as big as an old tomcat, while his little cousin is only the size of a half-grown kitten. In one respect, however, they are equals—they fear no one. Each is heavily armed and a deadly shot. Coyotes occasionally kill them but often live to regret it. Sometimes a hungry skunk will dispute a kill with a coyote or a bob cat, and the entire skunk family will feed at leisure before the larger animals or other scavengers may have their turns. William Brewer told an amusing story of five shirt-tailed men with blazing revolvers trying to drive one determined skunk from their commissary in the middle of the night. The poor skunk was finally done to death, but only after the camp had been so desecrated that it had to be abandoned along with a quantity of equipment and supplies.

On an evening in early August, Ruth and I took our sleeping bags into a grove of redwoods along the Big Sur River to spend a night beneath their towering branches. In this way, I thought we might feel their mood—we might enter into a communion with the primordial mysteries which the redwoods, above all other trees, embody for me. These magnificent trees came out of the cycad jungles of the ancient Jurassic period. Their ancestors contributed heavily to the great coal deposits of the later Cretaceous period, and the amazing species survived all of the turbulent Cenozoic era—Paleocene, Eocene, Oligocene, Miocene, and the glacial Pleistocene. After 50 million years of existence, the redwoods are truly a living fossil.

The isolated groves of the Big Sur redwoods are the extreme southern outposts of this unique forest which remains (and struggles northward) along 500 miles of the west coast United States. The east-west dimension of the forest is seldom more than a few miles, since the lateral range of the Coast Redwood corresponds to the coastal fogs which in summer creep up the mountainsides or wander inland along the river valleys. During Cenozoic times, forests of the same and closely related species

88

*Redwood, Palo Colorado Canyon*

extended around the world in the northern latitudes. Of more than 40 known species of fossil *Sequoias*, only these tall and slender California redwoods and the heavier-trunked "big tree," or giant sequoia of the high Sierra, continue to grow. Why this species has not survived above the Rogue River in Oregon is not clear; but it is possible that they were destroyed there during the later ice ages and have been unable to regain this range because of lower temperatures and the competition from the faster growing Douglas firs, hemlocks and red cedars.

Drowsing upon a thick mat of dry twigs and leaves, within a near-perfect circle of a dozen slender redwood trunks soaring without branches for almost 100 feet, Ruth and I found it inevitable that one begins to imagine secret things—to think of Druidical rites, of primeval monsters, of ancient, guarded knowledge. Of course, a certain amount of rationality and background information tends to remove this spell. We know, for example, that the redwood tree, like all other earth-bound organisms, is a creature of its environment. The mysterious "fairy rings" of redwoods, for instance, have a simple, even mundane explanation.

The redwood, a *gymnosperm*, bears winged seeds, which grow naked between the scales of the nutmeg-like ¾- to 1-inch diameter cones. Although these cones are produced in great numbers, the seeds seldom germinate. They fall to earth and are smothered in the deep dry duff beneath the trees. Only after a fire has burned away the duff, exposing mineral soil, can the redwood seeds germinate and reproduce readily. Fortunately, the redwoods, unlike most conifers, do not rely solely upon seedlings for its perpetuation. Both the redwoods and their relative, the bald cypress of southern swamps, produce sprouts from the stumps of adult trees. These sprouts grow rapidly, accounting for much of the reproduction. And this is the reason for the peculiar circular formations, the "fairy rings," in which redwoods are sometimes found. Once a huge tree stood in the smooth clearing at the centers of these circles. That tree eventually died, either from disease or from damage by wind or lightning, but not before it had produced a ring of vigorous sprouts about its massive base. Then, slowly, as the slim off-spring grew taller, the stump of the mother tree decayed and faded away, leaving after hundreds of years a ring of trees, all roughly the same size and age.

A peculiarity of the redwoods less easily explained is their tendency on occasion to revert to more ancient forms of growth. It is not unusual for seedling redwoods, or young sprouts, to produce some twigs bearing the juvenile, awl-shaped needles of their more primitive "big tree" relatives, the giant sequoias. At Lion Creek, on the Nacimiento road where we camped one night, Ruth and I discovered several mature trees which had produced, so far as we could see, none of the normal fern-like fronds and looked more like *gigantea* than *sempervirens*. I concluded that they must be "big trees" which had somehow found themselves far outside their normal range in the high Sierra of south-central California, though I was puzzled by the fact that the cones were only half as big as they should have been and the butts of these trees did not flare in the characteristic "big tree" manner.

Professor William Doyle, biologist of the University of California, Santa Cruz, settled the matter for me (although he did not entirely explain the mystery) by stating that "Trees with all or mostly scale-like leaves are not unusual toward the southern limits of the range of coast redwood, especially on older trees that appear to be under stress." Since the trees which puzzled us were growing with their roots almost within the water of Lion Creek, the "stress" Dr. Doyle referred to may very well have been an excess of moisture. As fog-belt trees, redwoods do not require large amounts of ground water.

During that night beneath the trees, a pair of raccoons came ambling into our sylvan sanctuary and nosed about among the fallen leaves, searching no doubt for worms or the larvae of insects. Whether from lack of interest or disdain, they ignored us completely. It was peculiar— raccoons are usually more curious. There were no other disturbances during the night.

It was quite impressive, really. To think of the immense animal population with which we were sharing the night, and yet the forest was so still, so perfectly silent that we could not help thinking that the canyon was uninhabited and we were alone. Earlier in the season, we would have been assured of the haunting mating calls of the band-tailed pigeons which roost in the redwood canyons. But by mid-summer these handsome game birds, with their darkly banded, broadly rounded tails, had broken up into mating pairs and were quietly and inconspicuously nesting high in the branches of the madrone and sycamore trees along the river.

In the early morning, when we awoke, fog was drifting through the tree tops. Looking up I saw something I had not noticed in the evening's shadows. As high as one could clearly see, the grooved, fibrous bark of the redwoods was dappled with thousands, perhaps tens of thousands of large spider webs, each one of them shining with accumulated dew. I could not help but to hark back once more to my thoughts and feelings of the night before. A circle of sprouts and a dying mother stump may explain the redwood "fairy ring," but there was also something beyond rationality—something mysterious and magical—in these somber, dignified and magnificent relics.

The morning fogs, which ground the larks and mourning doves and keep the black-tailed deer "at home" in the shelter of the thickets, have little effect upon the denizens of the beaches and the kelp patches. Cormorants and pigeon guillemots nest on the very faces of the sea cliffs and probably find the rare hot sunny day to be far more discomforting. The 200 or more seals and sea lions out on Seal Beach certainly find the fog no damper on their enthusiasms. On mornings when we could not see beyond our noses, the pugnacious sounds emanating from the beach assured us that life proceeded there as usual.

The dozen or so otter which Dryden and I found at Smugglers Cove proved over countless visits to be an extremely relaxed and loose-knit clan or family group. We suspected that they were all the offspring of a single dominant male and a half-dozen adult females. The old dog otter who was the head of the family and father-image to all the clan was easy to recognize. He was large, well-fed and lazy. His chest and round head were almost white; his face was a grizzled gray; a bulbous, jet-black nose was framed in long white whiskers which drooped stiffly downward, giving him an "Ol' Bill" appearance. Heavy folds of skin hung beneath his arms, forming pouches into which he tucked his surplus food. When he floated on his back, his masculinity was more than apparent.

Several other adults had gray or white heads, but Ruth and I concluded from their behavior that the white was more a mark of ancestry than of age. One or two of the females were still accompanied by half-grown young which, like spoiled children, gave them little rest. There were five or six of these obstreperous youngsters and it was difficult to tell them apart or to determine which mother they belonged to. Generally, they played or slept together in a little raft away from the others, but when feeding time came they begged from their elders rather than to attempt to hunt for themselves.

Sometimes, although the adolescents were almost as large as the mothers, they attempted to nurse, or even to climb aboard her belly to be groomed or to rest. I was not sure that it mattered to them whether the "Mamma" sat upon was actually their own or only the female nearest to them. In either case, the cubs were old enough to have better manners and the adults told them so by pushing them off. (Young otter are called "cubs" at this age. They lose their designation as "pups" once they lose their wooly brown baby coats.)

There was only one "yearling" that I was able to identify all of the time—he had his father's patch of white hair upon his chest. There was also one adult female who could be identified readily from a distance because she was well-advanced in pregnancy. We gave her a name, "Kiska," after the bleak Aleutian island near which Dr. Steller first saw and reported these amazing animals. We also determined to keep her under careful observation in the hopes of seeing the birth of a pup—a happening which, so far as I know, had never been witnessed.

We had by now discovered that the Smugglers Cove colony was only one of many such small groups of otter scattered along the 150 miles of rugged coastline from Monterey Bay to Morro Rock. (One of our favorites for observation is just off Anderson Creek, a half-mile south of our tent camp at Waterfall Cove.) No doubt they hunt all the reefs and kelp patches of the area, but they tend to gather for rest and community into small colonies spaced a mile or more apart. I suspect that these congregations, like the one at Smugglers Cove, are actually extended families held together to some extent by their kinship. So far as we could tell there was little exchange between colonies, but I assume that the young adult males must wander quite widely in search of mates.

Without the necessity to travel far for food, the sea otter seem to have lots of time for sleep and relaxation. I never learned when they went to sleep at night, but I frequently arrived before they had awakened in the morning. They usually slept singly in the kelp or in small rafts of several individuals at the edge of the kelp patch. ("Raft" is used with otter in the

W. F. Bryan

*Mother otter and cub*

same way that "pride" is used for lions or "covey" for quail.)

The young adults most often rafted together. Mothers and cubs also slept side by side at times, and occasionally the old harem-master would be found sleeping together with two or three of the adult females. More often, he slept apart, generally at the far edge of the kelp patch. On rough days, the entire colony would sleep together in a tight raft which somehow held together without any apparent attempt at organization. Regardless of the weather, the otter slept on their backs, their arms across their chest and their hind legs and tails usually folded forward across the belly.

If one might judge from the amount of stretching and yawning that went on in the morning, the otter sleep quite soundly at night. During the day, after feeding and grooming, they often slept again, but this time by fits and spells—with one eye open, as it were—either because there was more danger by day and therefore more necessity to be alert, or simply because they had had more than enough rest the night before. On the whole, the otter life was most casual and unregimented, with little of the stress exhibited by many wild animals. Once they were awake (usually shortly after dawn) and had stretched, yawned and scrubbed vigorously with their paws, they would roll over and swim to the nearest rocks to feed.

If the tide were low, mussels, barnacles, urchins or crabs could be taken from the face of the rocks. More often, the hunting had to be done beneath the surface. Sometimes several urchins or clams were tucked into the pockets of loose skin below the arms, and the otter would then return to the kelp to breakfast at leisure. Crabs were too active to hold in this manner and had to be dealt with immediately. A big crab, especially, presented quite a problem. He had 10 legs and 2 claws and a tremendous reserve of strength and determination. The otter had only two paws, plus some sharp teeth, but a big crab was obviously a choice morsel and worth a bit of a struggle.

Holding the crab between his paws, the otter would tear off the legs with his teeth and store them one by one in his armpits. And here we noticed a peculiar thing: In nearly every instance, objects were tucked first into the left armpit. When it was full, the right might be used for the overflow, but apparently most sea otter are right-handed. After devour-

Ann Bryan

*Otter eating Squid*

ing the contents of the carapace (often with the help of a neighbor), the otter would crack and pick the legs in a more leisurely fashion. At frequent intervals during the feeding, the otter roll over in the water—a convenient means of brushing the crumbs away.

Whereas most carnivorous animals fight over food, the sea otter actually shares it, and not only with members of its family. In unexplainable ways the neighbors usually know when a good catch has been made, and they feel free to join in the feast. I remember watching a female otter one evening as she dived and hunted near the shore. She had caught and eaten a number of small crabs and urchins when, after a dive much longer than usual, she surfaced with a fairly large abalone under her arm. No sooner had she begun to enjoy her meal than another otter came swimming around the north corner of the cove, fully 50 yards away. It was an adult, or nearly adult, but I did not determine its sex or have any way of knowing whether or not there was a family relationship between the two.

By then, the female had torn a chunk of flesh as large as a man's hand from the mantle of the abalone. She held it between her paws as she devoured it, leaving the remainder of the abalone on her chest. The newcomer took it without hesitation and with no apparent protest from its finder. Later, the visitor handed back the shell—and I believe it was deliberately "handed" and not taken. The female dropped the shell overboard, and the two groomed themselves contentedly.

How did otter number two, who was at least 150 feet away and out of sight beyond the point of rock, know that its friend had taken a fine big abalone—and that it would be welcome to share in the feast? Was the neighbor invited to dinner or did he just drop in? I have no certain answers, but I suspect that there was some kind of communication, though it may have simply been the incidental communication of random sounds carried under water. Sounds do carry readily through water, and the female may have been chattering happily to herself, or perhaps the mechanical sounds of the abalone being pulled from a rock carried to the second otter.

As to the ready sharing of food, it may well be, of course, that otter number two was a relative, perhaps even a grown-up cub of the female otter. Still, the sharing of food seemed quite common, and I have never seen a sea otter fight over food. They will not even tangle with the gulls, who are always dogging the otter's steps while feeding and will steal whatever they can. Otter obviously find the thieving gulls a great nuisance, but the only defense I have seen employed against them is avoidance.

During the late afternoon feeding period at Smugglers Cove, most of the hunting was done off shore. Usually the otter would stand high in the water and look about him—perhaps to be sure of his bearings, perhaps to be sure that no enemy was near. Then he would arch his back, press his forelegs rigidly to his sides, and dive with powerful strokes of the paddle-like hind paws. Most of the diving was within the kelp, where depths are not over 60 feet, but otter are known to dive more than 100 feet at times. The otter remained underwater usually less than a minute, and often several dives were made in order to retrieve one elusive crab or tenacious abalone. Some dives in deep water were more than two minutes in length, but these were rare. By dusk, the otter return again to shore and continue feeding along the rocks or in the shallow waters of small coves and inlets.

Always after feeding there were elaborate grooming sessions. This grooming process is not just a sociable pastime. Rather, it is of utmost importance to the sea otter; for the animals are dependent upon a thick, healthy, clean coat of fur to keep them warm and afloat. When the fur becomes matted (often from oil or other pollutants), it loses its ability to trap air and, therefore, its buoyancy and insulating quality. Water temperatures along the Big Sur, even in summer, are usually in the low 50s, and an otter's body temperature must be kept close to 100 degrees. Thus, if the fur is not cleaned, the animal can die of exposure, exhaustion or drowning.

At times in the otter colonies in the area, there was a certain amount of what appeared simply to be visiting around. Within the Smugglers Cove community, for example, an otter would swim leisurely from one group to another, pausing for longer or shorter periods of time to chat. This "gossiping" was never very animated, and only on still days could I overhear any sounds. Those sounds—the sea otter voices—are difficult to describe. The first time I heard them, I mistook the sound for the mewing and cackling of gulls. But the otter have several other more distinct sounds: sometimes a shrill "eeeech," or a chittering sound like a squirrel's bark; sometimes (and I noted this later after Kiska's pup was born) a soothing and contented clucking and chirping between mother and child.

Occasionally, one or two otter would leave the Smugglers Cove family group, swimming away suddenly (usually southerly) as if upon a prearranged plan. Once they had disappeared around the point of the cove, I was unable to follow them, and I was never certain when they returned. The next morning when I returned to the cove, the entire colony would be intact again.

They made these southern excursions, I think, both because there were miles of rocks in that direction and good feeding grounds and because there were other colonies of otter to visit. To the north of the cove there were few offshore rocks or sheltering inlets and, therefore, few if any otter colonies. To the south, of course, was the Anderson Creek group, as well as three miles of good hunting waters. We often saw individual otter working this middle area between Anderson Creek and Smugglers Cove, and I just assumed that visiting between the two groups is fairly commonplace. As we were to discover later, this middle area around Waterfall Cove also provided an ideal "lovers lane" or trysting place for otter from both colonies.

I went several times a day to Smugglers Cove to observe the trend of events and, especially, to be on hand when Kiska bore her pup. Mornings were still wet and chilly, although the rest of the country was sweltering under a mid-summer heat wave. By noon the fog had been absorbed into the warming air, and the sun beat down into the tight-walled cove. Returning from a morning of fishing, a pair of snake-necked cormorants drooped over the tidal rocks, fluffing their wet wings. A cluster of gulls atop a higher rock were unusually calm and quiet, enjoying the warmth radiating from the granite cliffs. Far out at sea, a stick of pelicans floated by. As such days passed, Ruth and I became more and more eager for the happy event that must soon take place.

Each day as evening approached and hunger began to reassert itself, the otter always became more active. But we noticed one day that Kiska, the expectant mother, no longer took part in the feeding. Instead, she lay a little apart from the others grooming herself. She licked her forepaws one finger at a time and then pulled her hind paws forward to do the same for them. This she found difficult because of her enlarged belly. When she held a hindpaw between her forepaws and tried to reach back to scrub with her tongue between the toes, she would rise so high in the water that she became top heavy and fell over. Finally, the only way she could reach the hinder parts was to roll into a ball and perform her toilet underwater. This grooming and vigorous abstinence went on for several days. She waited and we waited. Then it happened and we had missed it.

At first glance, nothing had seemed different that morning. I had gone down to the cove after a hasty breakfast. No one was upon the road. Dew hung heavy on the shrubbery along the narrow trail and the scent of sage was strong. Partington Creek babbled contentedly in hushed tones. A benevolent silence pervaded the small stand of sorrel-carpeted redwoods beyond the stream.

Coming out of the tunnel, I noted that the sun had not yet reached the inner cove but sunlight danced brightly on the small waves beyond the kelp patch. The otter seemed to be in their usual places, though I did not immediately attempt to observe them closely. I thought it would be another warm and lazy day, so I made my way across the rocks, passing the ruin of the ancient tanbark derrick, and then settled into my accustomed resting place near the northern point of the cove. Only then did I unsling my field glasses and begin a careful survey of the scene.

Every otter seemed present and accounted for. Some were still sleeping soundly on their backs, their forepaws over their eyes or folded demurely on their chests, their flipper-like hindpaws drawn forward across their bellies or sticking up grotesquely like those of a dead animal. Others were feeding, and a pair of young otter, apparently already well-fed, were playing together at the outer edge of the kelp.

I located the old sultan almost immediately. He was resting as usual in an open spot among the fronds of kelp, his tail folded forward across his grizzled belly and his huge paws dangling listlessly in the air. But it was some time before I discovered Kiska. She was lying alone at the far right side of the kelp, at least 100 feet from her nearest neighbor. But she was not entirely alone, for I noted immediately that she had a baby on her chest. I set up the spotting scope and focussed upon her.

The pup was wooly brown, the size and shape of a small muskrat and about the same color. Even at X40 magnification, I could not make out its eyes or its ears. Kiska held the infant in her arms almost as a human mother would. She was gently licking its tiny face. It must have been only hours old. If I had arrived at dawn, as sometimes I did, I might have been witness at its birth.

For the rest of the morning, I concentrated on the mother and her pup. Apparently, both were exhausted from the ordeal of birth. They seemed content to rest while nature made whole the hurt of parturition. They did not move from the area and no other otter approached them.

Finally, after an hour or two, the pup wriggled free of its mother's arms

and sprawled across Kiska's stomach, finding the teats on her lower abdomen. While her infant nursed, Kiska groomed its stubby tail, its hind legs and all its afterparts with her paws and mouth. The day had grown very warm, the sea remained calm, and I had not brought my lunch. I hurried back up the trail to tell Ruth the good news.

One summer, when Dryden and Margaret Phelps were in India for a year and their Partington Ridge cottage had been rented to strangers, Ruth and I decided to "rough it" for the few weeks we would spend in the Big Sur. We arrived well-equipped for camping and had the good fortune of selecting a site which turned out to be so idyllic that we have returned there again and again, in every season. The site, a headland meadow above a 200-foot cliff, lacked the vast seascape of 1,000-foot Partington; but the view of sea and mountains was unobstructed and continually breathtaking.

We called the place Waterfall Cove, because the tiny, nearly land-locked bay below the cliff received the tumbling waters of McWay Creek, some 85 feet up the cliff. The sound of falling water was constant and comforting, and the view below the cliff-side barrier was one of unbroken calm. Even on stormy days, when waves thunder and break high on the outer rocks of the inlet, the waters of Waterfall Cove are hardly disturbed.

Behind us, across the highway, the chaparral covered the lower slopes and harbored a lively community of birds and animals. Above the chaparral, the mountain meadows swept upwards for thousands of feet, until they merged with a fringe of timber at the summit of the range. Each evening before dark, we would search these upper slopes with our glasses for signs of life, but generally there was little activity visible from that distance. Occasionally, we saw wild pigs or the mule deer high in the meadows. And, of course, there were always the small brown brush rabbits bounding about. When the sun finally set, it was an indescribably beautiful moment. Just as the red ball of the sun was about to sink into the sea, a marvelously mellow light slanted across the southern slopes of the ridges and set the pale grasses aflame with the deepest gold.

During a visit to Waterfall Cove by our son Ken, and by John Carson, his good friend, we three men determined to spend a day finding a way

*Waterfall Cove*

down the 200-foot cliff to the cove. I had always wanted to reach the plunge basin at the foot of the waterfall in order to examine the cavern behind the falling water. The assistance of the two able-bodied and experienced climbers, plus their considerable enthusiasm for the project, convinced me we ought to give it a try. Thus, early one morning, while the boys finished breakfast and prepared our gear, I went ahead to examine the cove more carefully for the safest way down.

From my vantage point just below our camp, I looked west upon a bold headland that forms the cove's embracing northern arm. There, the cliff rises as a sheer wall above the sea. The lower 10 feet of the cliff, the inter-tidal zone, is bald and barnacle-encrusted. The cracked and eroded granite beyond the reach of the highest waves is only slightly more inviting, with a garnish here and there of tufts of grasses and wild flowers or an occasional hardy shrub. Above this sharp rise, there is a fairly level shoulder of perhaps a half-acre, with a surprising variety of trees growing upon it.

The most conspicuous of these trees are the rugged, wind-swept Monterey cypresses, a species peculiar to this coast. There are also dark Monterey pines and some smaller live oaks and madrone trees. But the most unusual of the trees for this site are the tall, blue-gum eucalyptus and several ramrod-straight date palms. I have been told that the latter semi-tropical species were planted on the cliff many years ago by the Lathrop Browns of St. Louis. The Browns had for a few years owned the 1,700 acres now comprising the Julia Pfeiffer Burns State Park, and they had built a vacation house and planted an extensive garden on this point. The house has long since been removed, and the garden, except for these few exotic trees and some oleander bushes, has reverted to nature.

Above this bench with its graceful trees, there is another steeply eroded slope, scantily covered with grass and shrubbery, which sweeps upward to the summit of the cliff. An old switchback trail leads from the summit, where I stood beneath the laurel trees, down to the shoulder where the Brown's guest house once stood. That trail appeared to be the end of the line, however. I could see no way that the cliff could be scaled with our simple equipment.

I turned my attention across the cove, to the south. Saddle Rock, so-named because it resembles a low-cantled Mexican saddle, forms the left-hand encircling arm of the cove. The rock is virtually an island. It is attached to the sheer face of the east wall of the cove by a flying buttress of granite which arches 80 feet above the narrow beach and is no more than three feet thick in some places. Between these two granite thumbs lies the cove's narrow gateway to the open sea. And directly opposite this entrance, more than 100 feet below, McWay Creek plunges over the cliff in a sheer 85-foot fall.

To the west and south, the green sea water surged tumultously against the cliffs, but inside the cove there was serenity. The little bay was empty except for two small black rocks almost in its center and a surrounding patch of floating kelp. There were no otter in Waterfall Cove that morning. In fact, none lived there, although one or two would appear now and then to hunt along the cliffs or to splash in the plunge basin below the waterfall. Occasionally, sea lion also came into the cove, attracted, I think, by the splash of the waterfall.

I, too, was attracted by that waterfall, but I was no longer optimistic about reaching it. Confronted with the reality of that proposed descent, I realized that it was probably much beyond us and our equipment. When the boys joined me cliffside, we consulted about the possible routes down and quickly agreed that Saddle Rock was the most promising—in fact, the only possibility for us.

With a coil of stout nylon line, Ken, Johnnie and I set out. From the southern edge of the cliff above the falls, it was impossible to see the point where the slender buttress joined the wall to Saddle Rock. However, we knew it was there, some 30 feet below us, so we attached the line securely to a cypress tree a few feet back from the brink and prepared to descend. Ken volunteered to be the first over the edge. He disappeared with a terrible rattle of falling rocks, and a few seconds later, he had his feet on the bridge. Then, still secured by the rope, he made his way on all fours across the narrow archway to Saddle Rock.

When he was on safe ground atop the Saddle, Ken secured the line and motioned for Johnnie and me to follow. We rechecked our end of the line, for it was clear from the falling rock that the cliff was too soft and rotten to allow us to descend or return without the rope. (Any climbing on the cliff is now forbidden as extremely dangerous by the state park authorities.) With the rope well-knotted, Johnnie and then I scrambled down the cliff quite quickly and joined Ken on the Saddle.

We spent more than an hour examining this bleak, wind-swept rock upon which life is waging a last-ditch stand. On the north shoulder, below the flat-topped horn of the saddle, one small, isolated patch of soil remains. It is no broader than the average suburban patio and it can not be more than a few feet thick, but it supports a fascinating microcosmos of remarkably hardy plants and animals. We only had time that morning for a sketchy survey, but I have since speculated often upon the intricate relationships, the highly involved web of competition and dependency, the desperate struggle for survival which must go on within the limiting boundaries of this island of earth.

The fragment of soil had a spare groundcover mainly of mosses, lichens, brackens and the occasional lupine or salal. A half-dozen dwarfed Monterey cypresses were growing from this shallow patch—the tallest of the trees no more than 30 feet. Each of these gnarled veterans bore its associated camp of lichens, fungi, mosses and insects. We saw no signs of nesting in the battered cypresses. We also found no four-footed animals resident upon the rock, though it seems likely that there must have been a few pairs of publicity-shy shrews or field mice living there.

The many dead branches of the trees, bared and silvered by wind and spray, were covered with a red, moss-like growth which I had never seen before. Nearby rocks also had the strange covering, which upon later examination in a botany lab, proved to be a green algae. Unlike the gray "goat's beard moss" which the algae resembled (but which, despite its common name, is a lichen), this growth is green during the moist seasons of rain and fog but turns a bright henna-red in the dryness of midsummer.

Aside from this patch of life, there was little to observe on Saddle Rock. An oyster catcher stood watch for crabs on a fringe of sand below us. A litter of clam shells, empty tests of sea urchins, and fragments of crab legs indicated that if we were to wait long enough, we would be joined on the rock by a group of feeding gulls and crows. The boys shifted their attention from nature studies to a route to the beach, but they soon concluded—and I heartily concurred—that without another rope, there was no way we could make the descent safely. Slightly frustrated by our short-lived adventure, we worked our way back across the narrow stone arch and scrambled up the rope to join Ruth for lunch.

Although morning fogs generally continue through the month of Au-

*Vine in moss*

gust, the long summer drought begins to take its toll even in the lowest meadows. The daily bath of air-borne moisture is no longer sufficient to keep the wild grasses green, and the yellow of the dormant meadows moves swiftly down the mountainsides toward the sea cliffs. At the southern and hotter end of the Big Sur country, toward Pacific Valley and Piedras Blancas Point, golden meadows eventually lay side by side with the emerald sea. From Kirk Creek north to Carmel, verdant reminders of the lush springtime remain only in the cool moist shade of the redwood canyons and in the olive hues of the chaparral's oak and sage.

At this time of year in the Big Sur, no one can really say whether the season is late summer or early autumn. The earth is dry, the grasses are browned, and leaves begin to collect in crackling drifts beneath the trees. Yet, one also finds late-blooming flowers everywhere. And although land birds are generally quiet during these warm days, dutifully preoccupied with grooming and training their young, the song sparrows and scrub jays continue to twitter and scold in the chaparral as if it were still spring. At the shore, the sea fig, the sand verbena, the bluff lettuce and seaside daisies continue to bloom profusely.

On the other hand, there is an autumnal air of serenity and of muted changes in the Big Sur at this time of year. As certain evidence that the seasons are turning, flocks of shore birds begin to arrive daily from their northern nesting grounds. And yet another sign of the coming autumn: The rubbery nerocystis, or bull kelp, being an annual, begins to wither and break loose from its moorings. During the earliest sea storms of the winter months, these ugly, decaying tangles of kelp pile high on the beaches, where they incubate hordes of juicy sand hoppers to feed the foraging sea birds.

With this annual shrinking of the bull kelp patches, the otter are forced to feed and rest closer to shore. Since Ruth and I are fascinated and immensely entertained by these creatures, we took advantage of their closer proximity to the shore during this season and spent nearly every day at a lookout near the Anderson Creek otter colony, which was a half-mile down the beach from our Waterfall Cove campsite. Each morning we would walk at a leisurely pace along the sea cliff just as the fog was clearing and a warm sun had exposed the calm and empty expanse of blue sea.

Along the way, we would inhale the moist, heavy smell of sage and laurel and enjoy the perfect calm of these perfect days. We scanned the water for activity but were seldom rewarded with a sighting. Once we were delighted to discover an ocean-going ship passing by along the far horizon, and occasionally a small fishing vessel lay, or slowly cruised, near the shore. Sometimes we caught a glimpse of a seal or a sea lion on a hunting expedition. More often, we would spy the small bursts of white water created by leaping dolphins far offshore.

When we arrived at our viewing spot at the edge of the sea cliff near Anderson Creek, we were invariably greeted by a pair of irascible jays in a nearby cypress tree. Within arm's reach of our makeshift seats, a group (perhaps a family) of scaly lizards basked fearlessly on the warm rocks. Often, they would remain there at our side, sleeping or doing lazy push-ups, throughout the afternoon. This site was ideal for relaxed viewing of the natural world of the Big Sur country and particularly of the colony of otter on the kelp patch below. Anderson Creek flows down a deep canyon and enters the sea at a narrow slit on the rock. High crags surround most of the creek, but on the north there is a flat-topped, brush-covered headland easily reached from the road and perfectly situated for our purposes.

I would lay out my notebooks and sketch pads while Ruth held a bird book at the ready for quick identification of the countless passing sea fowl. There were so many varieties of gulls, terns, murres, guillemots, and cormorants winging past or nesting on the cliffs and offshore rocks —and so many sanderlings, sandpipers, plovers, willets, grebes, curlews, oyster catchers, turnstones and phalaropes on the beaches below—that we could never have learned to recognize them all at first sight. But we continued to make game attempts and even tackled the problem of trying to name the several species of marine ducks swimming and diving in the cove.

The brown pelicans with their eight-foot wing span and long, expandable yellow-pouched bills, seemed to be more numerous than in previous years. We took it as a good sign that this great species will survive. For a time, the pelicans appeared doomed. Man's chemical contamination of the seas had affected many inshore species of fish, and the chemicals (mainly DDT) that collected in the fish seemed to be causing the pelicans

*North from Anderson Creek*

to lay faulty, thin-shelled eggs. Fortunately, with the use of DDT and other harmful chemicals either banned entirely or carefully controlled, the danger to the pelican seems to be lessening. And because pelicans live for many years and have few natural enemies, there is a very good chance that these wondrous birds will soon be numerous again along the Pacific shore. I certainly hope so—they are a fascinating and beautiful bird to observe. After years of watching them, I am still thrilled by their startling technique of dive-bombing for fish; or by their habit of flying in close formation just above the surface of the water, with every pair of wings slowly stroking in unison, then gliding, then stroking again precisely with the rhythm of the leader. The loss would be great if the brown pelican were to disappear from the western seascape.

For all of our devotion and daily attention to the Anderson Creek otter colony, one of the most interesting of our otter experiences occurred right in our own "front yard" of Waterfall Cove. Since the edge of the cliff over Waterfall Cove was but a few feet from our campsite, I always checked the cove each morning upon arising. But for week after week of our stay, nothing ever seemed to be happening there. For week after week, the cove slept serenely within the deep shadows of its surrounding walls.

Then one morning, as I was peering down the 200 feet to the fog-shrouded and watery stage below, I discovered a lone otter lying within a bit of open water surrounding the tidal rocks. I ran to the tent, told Ruth of my discovery, and we returned with the glasses to examine our new neighbor. Her size and small mammaries indicated a young but adult female. The delicately beautiful creature, quite dark in color and un-marked by any spots of white, was resting quietly on her back. She was not asleep, however, for occasionally she would yawn or scratch herself.

All that day we watched as she moved about, hunted and played for a time in the plunge basin beneath the waterfall, then spent hours grooming herself. At dusk, when we left her, she was resting again in the same quiet water beside the rocks. The next day and the next were the same, and we got the impression that she, too, was waiting for something to happen.

We were not long in learning what. A big, very sleek male otter appeared on the scene on the fourth day. I first noticed him that afternoon when a rising tide and a light northwest wind caused a moderately strong surf to begin breaking below Saddle Rock. The glistening black newcomer was rolling and diving in the roughest of the water. The little female was in her usual spot and made no outward show of being aware of her visitor. We wondered how long it would be before they "discovered" each other. (I was sure it would not take long, for I felt certain this was no accidental encounter.)

The male abruptly disappeared around the point but then worked his way back again and finally swam into the cove. He skirted the outer edge, past the waterfall, under water as much as above. He seemed to be intensely interested in examining every detail of the cove, but we never once saw him glancing toward the little female, who still rested quietly near the center of the cove. I watched her carefully through the glass. She was alert, but she seemed also to be consciously adopting a very "cool" posture.

Finally, the male reached the foot of the waterfall, and he began diving and rolling and setting up a terrific splash. The romance of the situation, real or otherwise, may have been influenced by my imagination, but this looked to me like pure show. Whatever the intent, it worked; for after a time the female put all proprieties aside and dived to within 10 feet of him. The two began to swim and dive together, sometimes in the plunge basin, sometimes almost under the falling water. On the surface of the water at least, there was no physical contact or signs of recognition. Sometimes, when both stayed under water for unusual lengths of time, we wondered what we might be missing. However, the otter always surfaced some distance apart after these extended dives.

I had made plans to go to Seal Beach the next day to check on the four or five female elephant seal I had noticed there among the several hundred sea lion; so after breakfast I drove off, leaving Ruth to keep an eye on the blossoming romance at Waterfall Cove. When I returned to camp in time for a late lunch, Ruth was puzzled and disgruntled. The two courting otter had played around the waterfall for a short time after my departure and then the male had simply disappeared for the rest of the day. Ruth reported that the female had then lain back and gone promptly to sleep. And when I looked down the cliff at dusk, she was still sleeping soundly on her pad, a frond of kelp wrapped around one arm. It seemed to Ruth a very odd romance.

*Cabin, Plaskett Creek*

The next morning, the suitor was back in the cove again and the two were feeding together. This seemingly casual daylight association went on for several more days, until we were beginning to lose interest in this affair which did not seem to be ripening into *an* affair. Then one morning, I looked down through the light mist and spotted the two sleeping side by side on the kelp pad. I called Ruth to look and our interest warmed again. That day, the otter hunted and fed together, sometimes sharing food by passing it back and forth between them. Again that night, they slept together in the kelp, her nose tucked into the pocket of his arm. And at dawn the following day, we found them playing excitedly in the plunge basin, diving and rolling together and performing the otter equivalents of "necking" and "kissing." Ruth put her arm around me and squeezed.

During the next few days, this amorous activity continued, with long periods of rest and sleep in between. Otter "kissing" is often a somewhat bloody affair, since the male, when mating, holds the female's nose in his teeth. However, this couple seemed more genteel in their lovemaking, and the female suffered only a sorely swollen nose. Finally, one morning we woke up to find the female sleeping alone again, and for a couple of days, she seemed to do little else. She would awake and groom herself, and we often saw her toying with bits of kelp or a small stone; but we never saw her hunt or feed.

Then, abruptly, the female too was gone. We supposed that she had rejoined the clan at Anderson Creek. But with no identifying marks aside from a swollen nose, we could not be sure. Several other of the females in the colony were also nursing the wounds of romance.

Summer—the *real* summer of warm, clear, silent days—comes to the Big Sur when the grass-covered hillsides are browned to the sea coast, when berries have ripened in the chaparral, when the forest leaves begin to wither and fall, when the yucca blossoms, when wild ducks arrive from the north, when coyote puppies are weaned and hunting on their own. It does not come overnight, as spring comes with the rains, but slowly as the sun burns away the fog and the sea winds die on the beaches. One feels the tempos lessen, the heat increase. One sees the fog disappear. And then one fine day—it may be August, it may be September—one says to himself, "This feels like summer," and looking about, he knows that it is. But not quite—there is always an overlap, a blending of seasons. After weeks of hot clear days, a misty curtain may move in from the sea and bring the Big Sur style of summer back again if briefly.

*Driftwood*

*Indian summer days*

# *Four*

## The Warm Golden Days

The stillness, the somnolence of the warm Indian summer are illusory. With the land plants in particular, these "summer" months of September and October are the time when plans are laid and resources are gathered for the next season's battle of survival. Nutrients are stored and bulbs and buds are formed. Within a bud's protective scales, a miniaturized new plant—twig, leaf, flower and fruit—is preformed and packaged and held ready for the rains and the new growing season. At the same time, roots dig deeper as the ground water continues to recede, strengthening the plants for the next year's drought.

The animal world is also busy during these months. Many spend all of their time collecting or simply overeating their foodstuffs so that they can survive the period when the weather is bad and supplies are short. Fledgling birds try out their new wings, and the buck deer polish their antlers for the autumn rutting season. This summer-autumn period is the breeding season for many of the larger land mammals of the Big Sur. The long gestation period for these animals brings the young into the world precisely at the season when the earth is most abundant and productive.

Thus, although the summer heat of September and October melts away the fog, hatches troublesome insect larvae, and stills the daytime activities of the chaparral and forest creatures, this season only appears to our careless human eyes and ears to be a time of rest and waiting. Actually, a vast amount of "home work" is being done during this season to prepare for the difficulties and the benefits of the coming rainy season.

In the high dry valleys of the eastern slope, the Indian summer days of September and October are often so hot that even the snakes and lizards take refuge from the afternoon sun. The same is true of the sun-loving magpies, which spend these hot days moping and grumbling in the branches of the live oak trees. Evening always brings cooler air from the mountains, so that life can expand and breathe again. The magpies flit from tree to tree  seeking food and diversion. The red-headed acorn woodpeckers also become exceedingly busy, gathering and hammering acorns into the empty racks and holes of their chosen oak tree.

On the west slope of the Santa Lucia, it is never so hot and dry. To a trained forester this fact is spelled out in the varieties and the distribution of the trees. Whereas pale green digger pines stand like desert palms in the upper San Antonio Valley, the deep green of the ponderosa pines crown all of the exposed ribs of the western ridges. The coast live oaks are scattered through both areas, but their leaves remain fresher and greener on the west side. The oaks are joined on the western slopes by the shiny-leaved and aromatic California laurel trees and by maples, alders, tanbark oaks and redwoods.

One night in mid-September, Ruth and I moved our camping gear high up the golden mountainside to the hot, dusty, nearly treeless country below Lion Creek on the Nacimiento Road. The elevation was about 2,000 feet where we made our camp beneath a huge live oak tree. Grazing cattle were black dots in the pastures far below us, but here all was open and silent and untrammeled. It was a wilderness, but a mild and gentle wilderness. We had decided to move mainly in the hope of seeing and hearing coyotes, which are extremely elusive creatures, even though they are numerous in this region. We also planned, incidentally, to observe the far more easily found deer.

We soon spotted a black-tail doe watching us from a safe distance. In a moment, but without haste or sound, she then moved into the denser cover of a small depression alongside our meadow. Toward dusk, other deer appeared, singly and in family groups, to graze along the edges of the canyons. These are the so-called mule-deer, a name apparently derived from their large ears. However, these are smaller than the robust Rocky Mountain mule deer and are better described as black-tail deer.

The black-tail subspecies is numerous along the Santa Lucia Range and throughout the Big Sur area. They range from the summit forests right down to the beaches, but they are most often seen in the open parklands above 1,000 feet, where they can rest in the thickets or under live oak trees during the heat of the day. The black-tails in the Big Sur seem mostly to be of the smaller Columbia subspecies, but in the field it is not easy to distinguish them from the somewhat larger California black-tail. Also, it is said that the two sub-species interbreed freely, so the distinction is probably academic.

Both types of mule deer have black on the tail, although some individual animals are only tipped with black. The underside of the tail is always white—a kind of white signal flag which is exposed most conspicuously when the animal is frightened or running away. Only the bucks have antlers, and these are shed completely after the rutting season in late autumn. Even then, the bucks are easily spotted by their larger size and more solitary ways. The antlers are forked rather than tined, as with the eastern white-tail and the American elk.

We saw many tracks of coyotes and their droppings near our campsite, but that night we neither saw nor heard any. Perhaps it was only that we slept too soundly, for they must have been all around us. On other occasions and in far less appropriate settings, we had heard them many times. It was a disappointment not to see any of the "howlers"—the coyote is one of my special favorites among the four-legged animals of the Big Sur.

The coyote is one of the most successful of all wild animals, if success can be measured in terms of ability to survive. Whereas his larger cousin, the wolf, and such competitors as the eagle, bear and cougar, quickly gave way before the heavy hand and ready gun of the human invaders, the "little wolf" adapted and not only survived but prospered. In many areas, coyotes are as numerous as they ever were, and they have extended their range into large areas of the northeast and the northwest where they were previously unknown. Many live within sight of Seattle, Portland and San Francisco, and hundreds actually live within the corporate boundaries of Los Angeles. Recently, they have also invaded Alaska.

Coyotes manage to survive in closer contact with human inhabitants mainly because they seem better able than most animals to adjust to the environmental changes brought about by man. For example, they adapt with ease to new types of food. Along the Big Sur, the coyotes rely mostly on reptiles, ground-nesting birds, rabbits and small rodents, with mush-

118

*Lichen on barn door*

rooms and wild berries for a vegetarian change of pace. In sheep country, the coyote will kill a lamb occasionally, and a farmer is always very foolish to allow his chickens to run free. In the hot farming valleys, coyotes also destroy many melons and tomatoes. In cities, they have been caught raiding garbage cans. Confronted by the hazards of the ranchers' traps, poisons and guns, the coyote counters with a foxy cleverness and big litters of resilient little puppies. Coyotes even go so far as to scratch dirt in a rancher's eye by breeding with his dog.

The misbegotten idea that wolves and coyotes, or even foxes, are cowardly creatures is a libel upon these cousins of man's best friend. A coyote may be sly, if the occasion requires slyness, but he is not craven. (Nor is any wild animal—a brooding hummingbird will defy any creature to touch her nest; a mouse, if cornered, will bravely hold his ground against any enemy.) Ruth and I once had a dog—his name was Oscar—who loved to chase deer or any other invaders all the way to the boundary of his self-established territory. Then he would return home, proud of his boldness and satisfied that he had done his duty. Oscar finally met his match one spring morning, when a big male coyote, with a heavy black ruff and beautiful brown and buff markings, trotted across the pasture below our house.

Oscar, who was bigger though not nearly as wise, saw the coyote and dashed out in bold pursuit. But the coyote did not run. Instead, he stopped and looked back over his shoulder. Oscar skidded to a halt at about 50 feet. The coyote may have said something—we were too far away to hear—but he clearly felt unthreatened as he trotted on without increasing his pace or changing direction, his beautiful black-tipped tail straight out behind him. Oscar charged again in full cry, but then again stopped suddenly when the coyote looked back. The same thing happened two or three more times. Then the coyote sat down facing the dog, and this time we were sure he said something; for Oscar began snuffling around in the grass, pretending he was hunting for some fierce mouse he might rend limb from limb. When the coyote finally continued on his way, Oscar did not follow.

Along the Big Sur and high into the Santa Lucia, coyotes range widely during most of the year. But after the mating season—January and February are the months of exuberant singing and moonlit romances—the coyote families establish definite hunting grounds. A den is dug in a hillside or between rocks on the top of a ridge, and the bitch settles in for a gestation period of 63 to 65 days. Usually there are six or seven pups, but 10 are not uncommon. While the pups are small, the father does most of the hunting—killing rabbits, quail, even grasshoppers if the hunting is poor. The food is brought to a point a few yards from the den and left; the mother will not allow her mate to enter the den. After about 10 weeks, the pups are taken out and taught to hunt for themselves. When the pups are weaned, the parents go their separate ways.

In most areas that he inhabits, and certainly along the slopes of the Santa Lucia, the coyote definitely is far more useful than hurtful. Even the complaining farmers and ranchers have many reasons to be grateful to coyotes; for they would lose tons of grain to the gophers and ground squirrels if the coyotes did not keep the rodents in check. The coyote belongs to the western landscape, and his high-pitched howl is to the lover of the wild the true "song of the west."

Another creature of the wide open spaces, equally maligned and equally essential, is the turkey vulture. "Buzzards" we used to call them in the East. On any warm autumn afternoon, several of these huge black birds can be seen cruising silently on their stiff dihedral wings. With their keen sense of aerodynamics, they ride the updrafts in apparently effortless flight, their only visible movement an occasional flutter of wing tips. Each pair patrols its allotted segment of sky, their baleful black eyes missing little within the several square miles of their territory.

On cold and rainy days, the vultures gather together in some hidden canyon or on their nesting ledges and wait. I have never discovered the local roosting ground in the Big Sur, but back East, these dismal havens, with the broken tree branches and lime-spattered grounds, were introduced to me by an ornothologist. I have seen 100 or more of these "buzzards," with their undersized naked red heads and huge drooping wings, huddled together in a mute and ugly assembly. In contrast to such appealing compound nouns as "a pride of lions," "a gaggle of geese," "a pod of whales"—not to mention "a melody of larks"—I recorded such a congregation as "a gloom of buzzards."

*Madrone bark*

Vultures are, of course, carrion birds, scavengers, the "sanitary corps" of the ranges. The object of their search is death. They can see a dead rabbit from a mile away and a dead deer from even further. Their acute eyesight also serves as a means of communication; for although each bird patrols its own range without interference from its neighbor, no sooner does one bird sight a feast and spiral down to enjoy it than others gather in from miles around to share in the good fortune.

The vultures maintain a remarkable balance between population and food supply. Normally, two or three eggs are laid by the hen vulture on a ledge of rock, a decayed log, or even a spot on the bare ground that she has selected to cradle her downy white chicks. But if food is scarce, the hen will produce only one egg, or none at all—it is as simple as that. No one knows how many vultures remain along the Big Sur—a few hundred at most. Perhaps with the fade-out of cattle ranching and with the diminishing supply of other wildlife, that is all the Santa Lucia ranges can support.

Unlike crows and magpies, coyotes and foxes, Big Sur vultures apparently have not yet condescended to "panhandling" along the highway for the rabbits and other small animals killed by passing cars. At least I haven't seen them so engaged. Perhaps because their big clumsy feet make them far from agile on the ground, they find automobile roulette too hazardous. However, in Mexico I have often seen the same species patroling the highway and even invading the main streets of villages and cities for their daily fare. Occasionally, the turkey vultures can be discovered at work along the Big Sur beaches, where a dead seal or a stranded whale provides a gargantuan feast.

During all of our stays in Big Sur, I always gave close attention to the sight of the vultures soaring high on the updraft. My hope was that one day my glasses would reveal the white wing patches of the rare California condor. Field guides still list these great scavenger birds as native to Monterey County, although the few remaining pair only occasionally range so far north. Like the vulture, the condor is a bird suited to the vast open spaces of the West. It has twice the wing spread (9 to 10 feet) of the turkey vulture and is the largest land bird in North America. We have never seen one.

The condor has no natural enemies except hunger and disease; yet man, who does not attack the species openly, is fast bringing it to the verge of extinction. In the past, many condor were shot by thoughtless gunners, and others died from poison put out for coyotes and bobcats. For a long time, egg hunters were also a serious threat to their existence. But in recent years, there has been rigid protection of the birds, and a condor reserve has been set aside for the few remaining pairs.

Yet, the species continue to dwindle away. The major problem is that such birds cannot tolerate crowding. Highways, airplanes, settlement, campers—all violate their sense of freedom. Also, the gradual elimination of deer, range animals, rabbits and other wildlife has removed their food supply.

Less than 100 years ago, on any sunny afternoon, one or more condor could be seen perched on a ledge or circling high in the blue above. And a million years ago, judging by the remains of several species found imbedded in the Rancho La Brea tar pits, the condor were much larger and even more abundant. In 1862, William Brewer first found a 30-inch wing feather and later observed the huge birds close at hand as they fed on the carcass of a dead whale. Today, one is extremely fortunate to catch a glimpse of one from far away. It appears that what has been done for the condor is too little and too late. Fewer than a score of nesting pairs remain.

On the warmest days, when the narrow, isolated beaches of the Big Sur shimmer under the sun, I discovered to my surprise that small groups of the strange, obese elephant seals from Mexican waters often haul out onto the hot, dry sand to join the noisy resident colony of sea lions or harbor seals. You can readily pick out the visitors from south of the border. The seals and sea lions are always engaged in constant and seemingly chaotic activities on the beaches. By contrast, the blubbery elephant seals—once they are settled—rarely move and seldom even lift their heads from daylight until dark.

At most, they might roll their enormous doe eyes about when one of the lions stumbles over them. Or in a supreme effort, they will flip a little sand over their backs to discourage bothersome flies. But mainly they remain stationary and sleeping, just slightly apart from their cousin species. Their daytime laziness actually has little to do with their girth.

Ann Bryan

*Female elephant seal*

The elephant seals are almost exclusively night feeders (as their exceptionally large—and beautiful—eyes would tell you), so they sorely need their 40 winks on the beach.

Largest of all of the seal family, the elephant seals were almost exterminated for their blubber at the end of the last century. However, since 1911, when they (with the fur seals and gray whales) were given protection by the Mexican government, these lumbering creatures have made a remarkable comeback. Now, there are large herds breeding on Guadalupe Island off Baja California, smaller rookeries on two of the Santa

Barbara Channel Islands, and a very recently established colony on Ano Nuevo Island, a few miles north of Monterey Bay.

The elephant seals I have observed on Big Sur beaches were all females. Where were the huge bulls, with their long, elephantine, prehensile snouts? No one knows for sure, but experts speculate that the gentle cows are serving as the pioneer settlers for the species as it gradually spreads its range northward. An occasional lone bull is sighted as far north as Puget Sound, and one was found a couple of years back in Alaskan waters; so perhaps the bulls do the initial solitary exploration and then the cows follow and make a selected spot their home waters. At some point, the bull and his harem must get back together, but no one I know of in "Alta California" has ever spotted a bull enjoying a siesta with his voluptuous wives.

The seal family, a fascinating group of marine animals, shares a common ancestry with dogs. The seals are descended from canine-like land mammals which eons ago returned to the sea. These creatures became strikingly well-adapted to the life of the sea, yet they remained air-breathers and must always return to land to mate and bear their young. The seal family is called *Pinnipedia*, meaning "fin-feet." The name refers to the fore and hind legs, which have retained their canine-like five-digit feet, complete with toe nails. However, these "feet" have become so modified that they are really highly functional fins.

There are three main groups of these fin-footed "sea dogs": the whiskered walrus; the short-necked, ear-less (actually only the outer ear is missing) harbor seals, which are almost helpless on land; and the long-necked and fully eared fur seals and sea lions, which are able to turn their hind flippers forward and locomote awkwardly but effectively on land.

Five species of the seal and sea lion groups are found along the California coast, but the walruses are a monotypic genus confined to Arctic waters. The popular names for the seal family members, in various languages, always follow along the lines of "sea bear" or "sea wolf" or "sea dog" or "sea lion." Looking down upon a beach covered with hundreds of these squirming, charging, wallowing bodies; listening to their barking and bickering; smelling the stench of the polluted sand on a hot summer day (as one may at several points along the Big Sur), it is not difficult to understand how these names have come to be coined.

Still, do not think that I would in any way slander these remarkable animals. They are as smart as their canine cousins. They are both lovably cute and sleekly beautiful. They are generally gentle creatures. And in the water, no animal moves with more ease and grace. During ocean crossings, I have seen their round brown or black heads and their big curious eyes more than 1,000 miles from the nearest shore. Like the whale family, the fur seals are migratory and never appear lost or out of place amidst the loneliness and emptiness of mid-ocean.

I once decided to spend an entire early autumn day at Anderson Creek, arriving before it was light and remaining until it was too dark to see the water below. I thought it might be interesting to take note of everything I witnessed from one spot over several hours. The "spot" I selected was at the far edge of the Anderson Creek headland, where the land breaks sharply and drops straight down 80 feet to the sea. Below the cliff, within easy sight, are three small rocks about 100 yards offshore. And surrounding and extending its fringes even beyond the rocks is the kelp patch which supports the otter colony that would be the main focus of my 16-hour watch. The Anderson Creek raft of about 15 otter did not seem to be as close knit and stable a group as the one at Smugglers Cove, but I found the community extremely interesting, nevertheless, because two of the mothers there had pups.

When I woke on the chosen morning, my watch told me it was four o'clock. There was no glimmer yet of daylight, and I didn't wish to awaken Ruth or the boys; so I moved about without light as I dressed and rolled my sleeping bag to the foot of the cot. I had prepared my kit the night before: camera, binoculars and telescope, a walkie-talkie, sketch pad, pencils, flashlight, bird book, and my breakfast of an orange and a generous chunk of Ruth's nut bread. I planned to get water as I needed it at Joe's cabin (Joe being Johan Kooyman, a young Dutch carpenter who then lived beside the high bridge which crosses Anderson Creek). Ken's friend Johnnie would be bringing lunch and dinner to the site.

As I pulled a waterproof parka over my sweater and shouldered the pack, Ruth whispered, "Be careful." I kissed her and slipped out into the fresh, laurel-scented morning air. There was no moon and only the stars outlined the summits of the Santa Lucia Mountains to the east. To the west there was a black void, but I could hear the splash of the waterfall and the waves slapping rhythmically on the rocks below.

Walking briskly, I reached the bridge in 10 minutes and turned off the road. On the pavement I had felt the residual heat of yesterday and had had little sense of the mellow fragrances of woods and meadows and sea. But once I had turned onto the path, the air seemed to chill and grass and sage brush scented the moist sea breeze. As my feet felt for the narrow path through the low scrub, I could barely make out the two big cypress trees which stand near the north rim of the promontory. I approached the brink of the cliff cautiously, trusting more to sound and feeling than to sight. It was 4:35 a.m.

Sitting on the rude bench I had previously fashioned from two rocks and a broken plank, I spread my equipment upon the large cable spool which served as my desk. Then I composed myself and began to look about. I will quote directly from my notes of that day:

"The stars have begun to fade, though the silver orb of Venus still shines brightly overhead. There is the barest of an onshore breeze, and the warmth of the approaching sunlight is reflected as a pinker shade along the western horizon. I can see the summit ridges now, black against a paler sky. Except for the gentle tumble of water over rocks, there has been no sound yet from the kelp patch immediately below me.

"I can begin to make out the three offshore rocks, but only by the occasional splash of foam as a wave breaks over them. It is about half-tide. I can hear small birds twittering in the shrubbery around me, but as yet no sea bird has spoken. I know that cormorants and guillemots roost on the ledges not 10 feet below me and gulls most likely rest on the sea stack standing off the mouth of the creek.

"Now it is 5:00 a.m. and a song sparrow has begun to sing. I see gulls as white spots on the rock, and I begin to make out the darker outline of kelp on the water. I can barely see to read the notes I have been taking. I mount my telescope on the table. I should be able to see the otter soon. It seems to grow colder, perhaps because I am sitting still.

"The kelp is visible now, but it is impossible to distinguish the sleeping otter from the bundles of leaves and the black bulbous floats of the bull kelp. A gull dropped down from the rock. It is only a white spot on the water. Now I see otter. They are sleeping in several small rafts, tail to wind, 100 yards out. They are in about the same places they were when I left last evening. The first cormorants fly by, low on the water, heading north. I can see the offshore rocks quite clearly now. The tide is lower. It is going out. There are no seals on either of the rocks.

"5:30 a.m. There is a rosy glow in the notch above Anderson Creek Canyon, and light begins to reflect from the crests of the waves. The horizon is quite distinct now; there will be no fog this morning. Gulls and cormorants fly by, the long-necked cormorants in sticks of three or four close to the water. All fly north. I can see otter clearly, even without the glasses. No movement yet. Now one otter swims a few feet to join a neighbor. They touch noses, then lie still.

"At six I call Ruth on the walkie-talkie. She answers in a whisper; the boys are not yet awake. All is well.

"6:05. The Santa Lucia Range still lies in dusky shadows, but the whole sky above is an electric blue. The west is pink and mauve, the colors reflected brightly upon the water. The old, white-faced dog otter awoke, yawned, washed his face, and then went back to sleep, but the others are active now. A mother slips her pup off her belly and dives. The pup is rolling over and over, tangling himself in a frond of sea weed. The mother surfaces a few feet away with a rock under one arm and some shellfish under the other. She places the rock on her chest and begins whacking a clam against it. I can hear the sound clearly. The cub joins her. All the otter are awake now, and some are beginning to work their way north-ward.

"The second mother, the one with the smaller pup, is diving and feeding. She was down a very long time—two minutes, I think. In between dives, the pup is restless. He stands up in the water and looks for his mother. Then he attempts to dive but never manages to get beneath the water. Pups have to learn to swim and dive. Perhaps he is only looking under water for his mother. When she surfaces, he scrambles toward her.

"There are a number of gulls on the water now. They paddle about near the feeding otter, like little tugboats alongside an ocean liner. But they are not offering any help; they are thieves and beggars hoping to snatch an easy breakfast. The otter ignore them. Swallows comb the air over-head, so the insects must be awake also. The first mother and her cub are

W. F. Bryan

*Otter and Western Gull*

nearer shore now. The mother still holds onto her rock. I shiver and look eagerly for the sun. A big-eyed wood rat just ran over my foot and disappeared into a clump of sage and poison oak. I had a good look at him—more rounded and with softer fur than that of a house rat. The leaves on the surrounding poison oak bushes are green and scarlet, and the sticky mimulus is still in bloom.

"6:30. The sun is not up yet. 'Come on, sun, it is cold down here.' A large number of cormorants are now hovering over the water, diving and fishing just beyond the kelp patch. A flock of 'twitter birds' (I think they are sanderlings) flashed by like swallows just below the lip of the cliff. 'Come up, sun.' I'm watching the mother and cub who are feeding less than 100 feet out. She hands food to her cub and he whacks it on his chest just as his mother did. Is this instinct or only imitation? Suddenly, the cormorants leave and fly north in formations close to the water. The mother and cub begin working south.

"A small white fishing boat, with trolling gear out, is moving north along the coast about a mile offshore. Now the sun is touching it. Without great interest, I train the telescope on it. I can make out only one man who appears to be tending the lines. It is likely there is another man steering from the small pilot house forward. The thought comes to me that these men (and we who buy and eat their salmon) are just as much a part of this strange web of interdependence as are the sea otter, the dolphins and the pelicans. All of us fish in order to eat. All of us feed off the crest of an upward swirling stream of energy first set in motion by beams of sunlight upon the sea.

"I decide to climb down to the lower rocks at the mouth of the creek—I need the exercise and it appears that the feeding otter may pass close by the point of rock. The face of the cliff nearest the creek was steep, but not as sheer as the rocks below my lookout. Also, there were hand and foot holds to help me down. From an insecure stand on a rock only a few feet above the water, I waited; and soon the mother and cub swam by within 10 feet of me. I could, for the first time, see an otter youngster's eyes and ears and its stubby cat-like front paws. Otter pups look quite different from the adult animals. The fur is usually browner and woolier, and the head seems rounder because of the wool. Like the puppy of a shaggy canine breed, the eyes and ears are almost hidden in the fur.

"The pair did not see me, and moved on calmly past the mouth of the creek. I climbed back up the cliff. The sun has touched the offshore rocks; it will be here any minute now. There is a silvery glow along the summits of the mountains. I am no longer so cold—the climb warmed me.

"7:00 a.m. Hurrah! The sun has just touched my back and I immediately feel its welcome warmth. Actually, the day is well-advanced. It is the mile-high Santa Lucia, only five miles to the east, that left me so long in the chilling morning shadows. All the otter have now left their bedding area, but I did not see the last of them go. I was distracted by two

Ann Bryan

*Harbor Seals*

passing freighters, one heading north, the other south. The northbound track appears to be about five miles out; the southbound much farther. The fishing boat seems to have hove-to several miles to the northwest.

"An otter suddenly surfaces just below me and is feeding on a four-inch leather-backed chiton. The animal appears too tough for even an otter to eat. The mother and pup are now working back from the south, about 100 feet out. Their feeding range so far today is no more than 500 yards. The mother is still diving and cracking clams upon her rock. I see other otter now, widely scattered, all quite active.

"7:30 a.m. Joe just left in his pickup truck, heading south. Henry Miller used to live in that old weatherbeaten cabin alongside the bridge. And Dryden and Margaret Phelps' son, Lyon, lived there for a time, writing poetry. Lyon told me that on warm evenings, when the sea was calm, he used to take his flute down on the rocks at the mouth of the creek and play for the sea otter. 'They loved it,' he said. Henry Miller makes no mention of the sea otter in his memoirs. His interests, I'm afraid, lay in other directions.

"7:45 a.m. Only a smudge of black smoke shows where the freighters have passed. The otter are returning to the kelp patch, rolling and grooming themselves. Their appetites were quickly satisfied this morning. It seems to be siesta time already. The white-faced male is back, too, though I did not see him return. He appears to be sleeping again, his paws over his eyes. I have never seen an otter with so much white. He is marked from head to chest, and there is gray all along his belly. There's even a touch of gray on the underside of his tail.

132

"The second mother, the one with the larger cub, is lying close by the male. She also has a white face, and there is a tiny tuft of white on the chest of the cub. He has his head tucked under his mother's arm. The other mother and pup stop to rest farther out. Neither shows any white markings. She is grooming herself now and the pup has climbed aboard, though he does not seem to be nursing.

"8:00 a.m. I am having breakfast and the sun is warm upon my back. I've removed my sweater. It will be a hot day—it must have warmed 20 degrees already. Under the sun, the aroma of sage takes on a greater pungency. A small scaly lizard, a swift, just appeared on a boulder only a couple of feet from my elbow. Now he is doing push-ups with his front legs. I wonder if he is trying to impress me. I toss him a crumb of bread, but the movement frightens him away.

"I just went to Joe's cabin for a drink of water. Swallows were combing the air over the scrub. Their deeply forked tails indicate that they are barn swallows. I saw their nests beneath the bridge. There were also several rufous hummingbirds working some red and yellow torch lilies (Uvaria) near the cabin. On the way back from the cabin, I saw a three-foot snake along the trail. I had only a glimpse, but it looked brown and slim, like a gopher snake.

"Back at the lookout, I can hear a low barking but am unable to locate the barker. A lone otter is working the surf near the offshore rocks. He caught a large red crab, broke it up and ate it quickly, rolling frequently to wash away the bits of shell. A dozen cormorants are also feeding in the area. They dive deeply and stay under almost a minute at a time. Then they surface 20 to 30 yards away from where they went in. Usually they have a small fish in their beaks, and they quickly gulp it down, head first.

"The tide is coming in now—the kelp fronds are drifting northeast. Most of the otter are sleeping, several with hands over eyes, some cheek to cheek. One is holding his paws together as though praying. I'm reminded of Edward Hick's 'Peaceable Kingdom.' I call Ruth on the walkie-talkie. They are having breakfast. All's well.

"It is now 9:45. A windless, cloudless, day. It must be 85 degrees already and it will get hotter. I scan the horizon; there's no movement in sea or sky. I just saw a splash of white. There's another. I think it is a whale spouting, or dolphins leaping. It's a long way out. The glasses revealed pelicans, diving for fish. From 15 to 20 feet in the air, they dive straight down and make quite a splash. But they don't go under as the cormorants and guillemots do. They seem to just scoop the fish up. I had seen one or two flights of pelicans earlier, flying low over the water.

"The otter that ate the crab has joined the others in the kelp. He seems excited—rolling, tumbling, scratching vigorously. He rubs his chest with both paws as though he is scrubbing a table. Then he works over his tail and all four paws with his tongue and teeth. Now only his rump is out of the water, his hips surprisingly broad, his pelvis and back bone showing prominently. He seems to be grooming between his back legs under water. One of the otter pups is winding and unwinding himself in a frond of weed. The master, Old Whitey, has drawn a wet leaf across his face and is continuing his sound sleep.

"It is after 10 a.m., a quiet time—no porpoises, no seals or sea lions, not even the big red jellyfish which I had seen floating in the kelp yesterday. Rusty song sparrows are moving about in the shrubbery, but they have ceased to sing. I am getting sleepy myself. Perhaps the flooding tide will bring some action.

"Gulls suddenly set up a terrific squalling from a ledge below me, and several drop down upon the water. An airplane is passing overhead, but I don't think that's what set them off. More likely some domestic problem.

Now the lizard is back on the rock doing push-ups vigorously. He stares at me, or past me, then blinks his eye. Another lizard just appeared and chased him away.

"At 10:30, a strange otter arrives from the north and swims about from one group to another. Mostly the newcomer is ignored. I count 10 on the pad now. Some have lain still so long that their fur has dried and become fluffier and a lighter brown. I am half asleep myself. A monarch butterfly flutters past, and I notice for the first time a number of small white and blue butterflies working through the sage. Again, I call Ruth on the walkie-talkie. Johnnie will bring my lunch.

"11:00 a.m. John arrived with lunch and some cans of cold soda pop. He also brought a parasol to shade me from the hot sun. We moved back under the big cypress trees to eat.

"11:30 a.m. Back at the lookout just in time to see a large bull Steller sea lion pass by. He swims within 10 feet of a small group of sleeping otter, pauses to look at them, then swims on. He is heading south. The otter show no interest or concern, although they wake up. Soon another sea lion passes. This one pays no heed to the otter. There are now 11 otter in sight. I don't know where the last one came from.

"12:05 p.m. Three more sea lion pass beyond the rocks, moving fast and heading south. Several cormorants and pelicans fly by, still searching the sea for fish; but the gulls all seem to be resting on the water, moving lazily with the currents. A pale moon—quarter phase, inverted—is rising over the head of Anderson Creek.

"12:30 p.m. The mother with the smaller pup has moved toward shore and is diving again. The pup is clearly worried when his mother is out of sight. He tries to follow her, dipping his head down and kicking up a small geyser of water; but he barely succeeds in wetting his ears. His coat of thick wool traps so much air that he is as buoyant in the water as a sponge-rubber ball.

"1:00 p.m. I went to Joe's again for water. There is still no wind. It is certainly 85 degrees now!

"1:20 p.m. Three or four gray dolphins pass about 100 yards beyond the kelp patch. They are not leaping, only the arched backs and sickle-shaped dorsal fins are visible as they break water to breathe. The otter must have heard them, but they show no interest. I believe that the marine mammals must be able to identify many other animals by the sounds they make in the water. They know very well without looking who are their friends and who are the enemies.

"3:10 p.m. It's been a long, lazy afternoon. I have been half-asleep and so have all my neighbors. The rocks around me are too hot even for my scaly friends to rest on.

"3:30 p.m. Ruth called on the walkie-talkie. They are resting also.

"3:40 p.m. I look to find Old Whitey missing; he must be off on an errand. The mother and smaller pup are gone too, but I spot them feeding near the mouth of the creek. Most of the other otter are still sleeping in small rafts. Now one of the adult males begins to roll and tumble, with fits of vigorous scratching in between. Something is biting him and he seems to be having trouble locating it. Examination of captive otter have shown that they have few external parasites, so most of the combing and scratching that goes on is because of matted hair rather than itchy skin. Still, this fellow must have a fellow traveler.

"Two more otter roll over and swim toward the offshore rocks. It is high water slack and all three of the rocks are awash. A welcome breath of cool air has begun to flow down the canyon. The mother and pup are back on the kelp pad. She has a small red crab which she is dismembering and feeding to her pup. Now he has scrambled aboard and is nursing while the mother licks at the empty carapace of the crab. The second mother and her cub are working the swirls of white water around the rocks, and all of the other adults of the community seem to be awake now and feeding over a widely scattered area around the kelp patch.

"A hefty Steller sea lion passes by going north. He is close into shore and I can clearly make out the full black mane which covers his neck and shoulders. He may be the big bull I noted heading the opposite direction just before lunch. Just now, three more Steller lions pass to the north. They have their rookery at Seal Beach about five miles up shore.

"Margaret Owings, who lives high on the cliff above Seal Beach and who has observed and recorded the activity there for the past several years, tells me that the rookery is inhabited in about equal numbers by the larger, lighter brown Stellers from the north and the smaller, darker, California variety. Usually there are also a few harbor seals and female 'sea elephants' on the beach. Often, as many as 300 animals compete for the limited area of warm sand below the cliffs. Adult Steller bulls usually preempt the tops of the larger rocks at the water's edge.

"The little pup has quit nursing, and he and his mother are playing with the carapace of the red crab on her chest. Apparently tiring of the game, she finally rolls over to dislodge her pup. He continues to play with the crab shell in the water as she grooms herself.

"4:50 p.m. Cooler. Not an otter on the pad—I can count only five or six in sight. The cross wind begins to make herring bone ripples on the patches of open water, and the fronds of kelp are reversing directions. The tide is running out. More sea lion pass, all going north. One swims within 10 feet of a feeding otter. They glance briefly at each other, then the lion moves on and the otter continues to whack two clams together.

"There are four otter in the surf near the shoreline rocks, including the mother with the older cub. The cub is trying to dive and he finally manages, with a lot of kicking, to go all the way under. His dives never last for more than a second or two, however; and if he is trying to catch anything, he is not successful. Even so, when he comes up, he sometimes rolls over on his back and goes through the whacking motions.

"There must be an abalone on one of the rocks near shore. While her pup has been rehearsing his dives, the mother otter has been working steadily alongside a rock for some time. She seems to be clinging to the rock with her fore paws while her hind legs and tail are swished about by the surf. Some of the wallowing in the surf appears more like play than serious hunting. Two otter swim in from the north, side by side, both on their backs, both whacking clams.

"Another sea lion passes close into shore. The cub stood in the water and looked at him but exhibited no fear. An observer at Point Lobos told me that he had seen otter and sea lion actually touch noses, so there is, on occasion at least, actual communication between them.

"5:55 p.m. Still no otter in the kelp; all are out fishing. There are many passing birds now. Small sticks of pelicans—wings beating, then pausing, then slowly beating all in unison—scull like rowers across the sky. I don't know their roosting places, but they all seem to be flying north. The cormorants, gulls and guillemots all roost on nearby rocks or cliff-sides. For the past half-hour, a lone oyster catcher, big as a crow and as black, has been poking about on the bit of rocky beach at the mouth of the creek. He has pale pink legs and a bright red beak as large as a gull's beak. The oyster catchers are solitary creatures. I have never seen more than two together at any one time, and usually there is only one.

"6:30 p.m. I call Ruth. Johnnie will bring me some supper. It is cooler there, too. All the otter are out fishing, all over the area. Some of them are under water at any given moment, so it is impossible for me to count them now. The old white-faced male is still absent. I haven't seen him fishing. Perhaps he has a secret place. Perhaps he only spends his nights here.

"Several gulls have congregated to gossip atop the sea stack off the mouth of the creek. I find it difficult to identify the several species there. Glaucous winged gulls are here in the winter, but most of them are said to go north in the spring. This group seems to be mostly western, California, and ring-billed gulls, but there is so much variation in size and color within a species (partly because of age) that it is difficult to tell one from another. Anyway, they all sound alike. The adult western gull is the largest, the ring-billed the smallest of the gulls we commonly see. The California also has a red and black spot on his beak.

"The pallid moon is overhead now. Joe is back from work and came down to visit with me. Joe is an interesting man. He builds wonderful ship models and is now building himself a new cabin above Burns Creek, which is about a mile south of here. He lives alone and spends much of his free time here observing the otter. After hours spent in this spot, he has found a number of 'faces' in the granite of the cliffs. He pointed out for me a profile of 'Queen Victoria' on the headland to the south of the creek, and nearby a huge, lop-eared 'bloodhound.' I note a curious resemblance between the two.

"7:15 p.m. Johnnie arrived and we shared some sandwiches and ginger ale. He decided to stay on with me until nightfall. The otter clan is beginning to return. There are four nearby, all feeding. The smaller otter pup is nursing again.

"8:05 p.m. The sun's disc has become enormous and vividly red. Now it touches the horizon and is sinking fast.

"8:10 p.m. The red rim of sun has just sunk into the sea and the light on the water is fading rapidly. There are already heavy shadows near the shore. Only six of the otter are in sight. The mother and older cub are still near shore, directly below me. I must lean over the edge of the cliff to see them, but I can hear her cracking clams. Another sea lion hurries north and a spotted seal surfaces briefly, looks about, and sinks again. In the darker water, I can now see small silvery jellyfish pulsing slowly along.

"The cormorants and guillemots are returning to their nesting ledges on the sheer face of the cliff below me. Some of the cormorant nests are situated on rocky shelves so narrow that the birds' tails hang over the edge. The guillemots, like the puffins, prefer nesting burrows in the thin layer of soil near the top of the cliff, or they find deep crevices in the rock.

"Old Whitey has not come in yet, but several of the other otter are back resting and grooming themselves. There has been little play among them today, probably because of the heat. Play seems to be associated more with spring, sex and rougher water.

"Now there is a pink glow over the water only far to the northwest, where the sun sank from sight. But there is still a warm golden light on the highest meadows. The canyons look like streaks of ink poured down the sides of the mountains. The moon is brightening in the western sky.

"9:00 p.m. I see my first star. More likely it's a planet, but I'm not sure which one. It is too dark to see clearly across to the kelp patch, but I can make out some movement and I hear whacking and occasional otter talk. The latter is hard to distinguish from the muted conversation of the gulls. The cormorants make no sound. It is quite cool now, and I am more than ready to call it a day. I did little, but the day was tiring nevertheless.

"At 9:30, Johnnie and I finally gather up the gear and head home. 'Tomorrow,' Johnnie quips, 'otter be another good day for us otters.' "

Exploring the arid upper slopes of the Big Sur can be a hazardous business if one is not informed about the properties of the countless yucca plants that decorate the landscape. One brush with the stiff, needle-sharp leaves of the yucca will convince man or beast that the species' common name of "Spanish bayonet" is properly applied. The tip of each yucca leaf is armed with a spine so sharp that it will penetrate a heavy boot; and in a thicket of yucca, these lethal little daggers overlap and point in all directions. The yucca patches serve perfectly as fortresses for the harried little people of the wilderness—the field mice, pack rats, ground squirrels and other small creatures which can slip under the spines and avoid the pursuing hawk or coyote.

The yucca family is large and widely spread across all the arid and semi-arid regions of Mexico and the Southwest. A relative of the palm, the yucca finds optimum conditions in the hot desert areas of Arizona and Sonora, where it is called the Judas tree and grows in forests in which some of the trees are 15 to 20 feet tall and 100 or more years old. At the farthest edges of its range, in eastern Texas and in Montana, the yucca is a smaller, though equally formidable plant about one foot high. This species lives only a season. As a child in Oklahoma, I knew the yucca as ''soap weed'' (in fact, the Indians made an effective detergent from its roots).

Along the Big Sur, the yucca grows from sea level to the edge of the summit forests. On favorable sites at low elevations which avoid the chilling fogs, the yucca's flower stalk may stand 10 feet tall and bear hundreds of waxy white flowers. The Spanish called these dramatic blooms ''candles of Our Lord.'' Each plant flowers once and then dies, though the stiff flower stalks may remain standing through the following winter.

There is an unusual, almost romantic aspect of the yucca's nature which the casual admirer does not see. This secret element in the life of the yucca involves a little white moth of the genus *Pronuba*. This species of insect (called ''yucca moths'') is so dependent upon the wild yucca that it cannot survive without it. And the yucca, too, has become almost totally dependent upon its insect friend. Each contributes an essential service to the other in a relationship which could serve as a definition of the term ''symbiotic.''

First of all, the moths spend their pupal stage (and the winter) underground. Then with exact timing—triggered perhaps by the same springtime warmth and moisture which causes the yucca to bloom—the insects emerge from their subterranean nests and mate. Immediately, the pregnant female flies to the opening yucca flowers and deposits her eggs deep within a bloom's ovary. Then the moth gathers a wad of the yucca's sticky pollen and smears it over the stigma of the flower, thus assuring fertilization of the seeds within the ovary.

In a sense, then, with services rendered, the female moth pays her family's board and room in advance. And having done so, she dies.

Meanwhile, as the seeds are developing within each ovary, the tiny, worm-like pronuba larvae begin to hatch and to feed upon the yucca seeds. From that point on, the yucca is paying for essential services already rendered, which would seem to be a self-defeating process.

However, the thing which has made it work smoothly for millions of years is that the yucca produces many, many more seeds than the greedy pronuba offspring can consume. The result: Healthy fat larvae eat their way out of the yucca seed pods, fall to the ground and pupiate. At the same time, the pods have opened so the remaining yucca seeds can be scattered upon the soil. These seeds will in due course germinate into new yucca plants, which will again grow and blossom just in time for the next generation of eager yucca moths and their hungry larvae. Biologically, this relationship of yucca and moth is the more remarkable because it is not merely between unrelated species of *plants* (such as that of the algae and the fungi, which produces the lichens). Rather, it bridges two exclusive worlds, plant and animal.

There could be countless further illustrations of the sensitivity of living things and the delicate adjustments that organisms will make to an environment. This is the meaning of ecology.

As the meadows and brush lands parch beneath the late summer sun and their grasses turn a golden brown, the hazard of fire in the Big Sur becomes a daily preoccupation of the human residents. They worry about their homes, of course, but the threat to the lovely, lush forest is even more frightening to them. It is years, sometimes even generations, before a forest will have recovered its health and beauty.

The chaparral is more resilient, which is a fortunate coincidence since this scrubby, dry "pigmy forest" is, of all plant communities, most susceptible to sudden, devastating ground fires. One hot summer day a few years back, a fire started along the highway near Gorda and swept up the steep hillside with the speed of a bounding deer. Within an hour, 100 acres of brushland had been blackened. It was a disheartening sight; yet within a very few weeks, wild cucumber vines had already spread a pale green ointment of leaf and stem across the blackened scar. And on closer inspection, I found that almost all of the trees and shrubs had sprouted fresh green stems from their charred stumps.

*Late summer sun*

In any forest, brush or grassland fire, it is often the animal population that suffers most. Many birds, reptiles and mammals are killed outright by the heat and smoke, but equal damage is done by the removal of their shelter and food supply. In a severe burn, even the worms and burrowing insects of the forest floor are destroyed as the humus is burned from the soil and the land is made sterile and desolate. Fortunately, the smaller animals, like the chaparral itself, display an amazing tenacity, and the biotic community can sometimes spring back into being with a rapidity that seems magical.

These small creatures which shelter and scavenge in the scrub are, in many ways, a marvelous group. As I've noted earlier, they occupy the bottom rung of nature's social ladder and seem to exist mainly to tidy the landscape, aerate the soil and provide an evening meal for the larger animals. The predacious animals—coyotes, foxes, ringtails, shrews, hawks, owls and even jays and magpies—are ever on the prowl, and most of the creatures upon whom they prey are the inexperienced young of the smaller and largely defenseless inhabitants of the brush and grasslands. The survival rate for all wild creatures is distressingly low, fewer than 10 percent of the small ground-feeding birds and animals can expect to reach maturity.

The "little folk" of the wilderness try to combat this heavy hand of nature with extraordinarily alert senses and a phenomenal fecundity. The ground-nesting quails are a good example. Whereas the swift-flying doves lay a clutch of two eggs, the quail will drop a dozen eggs. The adult quail are also blessed with the instinct to post separate lookouts while their large brood is feeding. At the first sight or sound of danger, one will cluck the alarm and distract the prowler while the other rushes the chicks into the nearest thicket. Similarly, adult rabbits and rodents may bear litters of six or eight as often as three times a year, and they boast extremely inquisitive and discriminating noses, as well as bright eyes and sensitive ears, alert to any suspicious movement or sound.

In short, the wilderness community operates by a system of checks and balances which gives the smallest creatures a fighting chance for survival and, at the same time, provides for offspring in ample numbers to fuel the survival of the large birds and animals. It seems a heartless system, that cannot be denied. But it is nature's own.

# Postscript

The Big Sur is a land of rare treasures. Some stand as bold as a grove of redwood giants or a spectacular golden sunset below a sheer and awesomely isolated granite headland. Many more are demure gems: dainty springtime blossoms on a hillside, an otter mother cradling her pup, the play of sunlight in a silent forest, shy fawns and covies of young quail venturing cautiously from the brush. Still others—perhaps the best—are even more hidden in the matrix of the whole. Among these are values to be felt rather than seen—to be known only by their spiritual worth, by their imprint upon our inner selves. These must be sought out, uncovered, discovered. it takes time and it takes desire. The speeding motorist never sees or feels them.

Our presence in the Big Sur has changed Ruth and me. Tuned deliberately for a few seasons to the mysterious rhythms of nature and to the abiding beauties of this chosen land, our lives were expanded and made infinitely richer. Night after night, we had slept beneath the star-filled skies on lonely ridges, under majestic redwoods and sturdy oaks, within the sound of falling water, beside the ever-moving sea. Day after day, we had watched, walked with, worried over, and sometimes talked with the birds and the animals—the blue jay in the scrub, the raccoon at our door, the passing whales, and the sea otter on their kelp patch.

And in the end, when we had to leave it all, we went away reluctantly, and with a greater reverence and appreciation for our natural heritage and for the sanctity of all living things. We also went away with the realization that nature's equilibrium is in a delicate balance, which man can nowadays too readily sway. If we are to find our proper place in the natural world, we must learn to walk *with* and not *on* or *over* the things that compose this complex and remarkable and beautiful world.

# Floyd Schmoe

Born on a Kansas farm, Floyd Schmoe came west to study biology at the University of Washington. He stayed on to become Park Naturalist at Mount Rainier National Park and later to teach ecology in the College of Forestry. With degrees from the University of Washington and from New York's State College of Forestry he has also taught at the University of Hawaii and lectured at a number of other universities.

During or after three wars he has taken time out to do relief and reconstruction work with Quaker service and United Nations agencies in Europe, Japan, Korea, and Egypt.

His extensive writing has resulted in numerous magazine articles and books. Other of his books are: *Our Greatest Mountain*, G. P. Putnam Sons, N.Y. 1925. *Wilderness Tales*, University of Washington, 1930. *Frozen In*, G. P. Putnam Sons, N.Y. 1930. *Cattails and Pussywillows*, Lake City Press, Seattle, 1933. *Japan Journey*, Silver Quoin Press, Seattle, 1950. *A Year in Paradise*, Harper & Brothers, N.Y., 1959. *For Love of Some Islands*, Harper & Row, N.Y., 1964. *What is Man*, Voyager's Press, Tokyo, 1970.

Professor Schmoe now resides with his wife near Seattle where their home overlooks Lake Washington and Mount Rainier. He continues to write and to enjoy his hobbies of painting and sculpture.